THE ONE MINUTE CLOSER

Time-Tested, No-Fail Strategies
for Clinching Every Sale

THE ONE MINUTE CLOSER

JAMES W. PICKENS

WITH JOSEPH L. MATHENY

**BUSINESS
PLUS**

NEW YORK   BOSTON

Business Plus
Hachette Book Group
237 Park Avenue
New York, NY 10017

Visit our Web site at www.HachetteBookGroup.com.

Business Plus is an imprint of Grand Central Publishing.
The Business Plus name and logo are trademarks of
Hachette Book Group, Inc.

Printed in the United States of America

First Edition: November 2008

10 9 8 7 6 5 4 3 2 1

Library of Congress Cataloging-in-Publication Data
Pickens, James W.
   The one minute closer : time-tested, no-fail strategies for clinching every sale / James W. Pickens.—1st ed.
      p. cm.
   ISBN: 978-0-446-54099-5
   1. Selling—Handbooks, manuals, etc. I. Title.
   HF5438.25.P5333 2008
   658.85—dc22   2008027726

Interior design by HRoberts Design

I would like to thank some very wonderful people whose inspiration and understanding made this book possible.

Lindsey Janell Pickens
Barbara D. Johnson
Gary Oelsen
William Davies
Josesph L. Matheny
Ralph Medeiros
and
all the master closers around the world
who contributed to this project.

Thank you again,
James W. Pickens

Contents

THE ONE MINUTE CLOSER

Author's Note

DEAR READER:

This is the last sales book I'll ever write. I want to thank you from the bottom of my heart for all you've done for me over the past twenty-six years. You have made my other books best sellers around the world, and have truly humbled me by your kindness and loyalty. This specialized publication contains powerful and intense one minute closing secrets I have learned from great master closers everywhere I have given talks. These wonderful individuals have shared their private sales and closing techniques, which I am honored to present to you. This little manual is written in part as fiction, and in a very easy to follow style. It contains exclusive one minute closing insights; and a particular wisdom all master closers adhere to. About two years ago, someone asked me why I would want to produce one more sales reference work, and the only answer I could think of was something I heard in Africa several years ago: "To give life to all that I have learned." A great master closer once told me, "It takes courage to be who you really are," and it took time for me to realize I am a closer and truly love the profession. In addition, to be able to put down on paper what others have taught me is truly a blessing. This book is different. It's intentionally written to be unique, to be novel, and to have a quickened pace. The one minute closing methods presented do work, and they will make you a lot of sales. All master closers know that "you never hitch a race horse to a plow because that would kill its spirit." I kept that thought in mind while writing, so in all honesty, this text is intended strictly to strengthen master closers and give even more power and spirit to those who have been given the gift of persuasion. I've been told privately that I could be risking some creditability by disclosing certain commanding "closes" and closing procedures. Well, I decided if I'm going to share (and, I hope, help others), and don't give everything I can, then I've given nothing.

So, reader, if you want to be a great master closer, then learn all you can from everyone you can, and pass it along. Again, I want to thank all those who believed in me and my work. May God always bless you, and from one master closer to another, the greatest secret in sales, that all-powerful and distinct element no one can destroy, is YOU!

Total success to you all.

Your friend,

James W. Pickens

Part I
Introduction

It takes courage to have faith,
and it takes faith to have courage.

—*James M. McCurley, New Orleans, Louisiana*

T his book is written for master closers by master closers, professionals from fifty-seven countries who wanted to share their secret closing knowledge and truths with other professionals, so they can become even greater masters.

The sales procedures and one minute closing tips contained in these pages have been gleaned from years of experience and success. Everything presented will help the reader increase his or her sales production by at least 25 to 35 percent. These "jump in sales" percentages have been proven and recorded over the past twenty-six years in actual sales practice and performance.

Most of the teachings disclosed are what master closers have privately kept close to their hearts and never before discussed or passed along to others.

This guide has a sharp focus and directness, with a very unconventional format. There is no story line, hype, or unnecessary sales dialogue. Just "go to" selling and closing facts, arranged in the order of a general international sales presentation. The unveiled closing laws and canons contained in this single-purpose source are unparalleled and not meant for new or timid sales-people, because anyone just starting out in sales would not have the negotiating experience to appreciate and understand half of what is being shared. The actual one minute closes exhibited in this edition have never before been in print. In fact, the closes presented are so dynamic they are guaranteed to get sales, time and time again. There is one close in particular that only a hand-ful of master closers have known about, and this one minute close is so effective that it will make most every customer who hears it purchase.

Now, the best way to begin this book is to first de-scribe the real and everlasting meaning of success. The reason is this: Every master closer who had input or contributed to this literary effort is, today, very prosper-ous and very successful.

The following document describing success was found in an abandoned monastery, located in the moun-tains of Mexico, and has been translated into English.

The Secrets to Success

The true secrets to success are not degrees from universities, association with the wealthy, applause from others, or wise business opportunities. The true, everlasting secrets to success are sorrows, disappointments, tears, frustration, and failure. Without these hurtful experiences, no man can honestly know himself, recognize his courage, or respect others. The pillars that support a man's character, stabilize his spirit, and strengthen his determination develop from adversities and heartache. Without enemies, how can a man cherish his friends? If a man's dreams are not obtained then how can he understand risk, or face suffering? All men have within them a talent that, when found, creates a boldness that attracts and encourages all, but to find that gift from God, a man must explore, touch the fires of doubt, and sip from the cup of pity. He must build on sand, be foolish, and scar the soul with pride. Then, when all is lost, all is found through a tried consciousness that has grown weary. It is at this point that a man silently reaches out, touches the fingers of hope, and acknowledges that his mansion of success is built on single blocks of stone carved with compassion and cut from quarries only God blesses with power and love.

This document just about says it all: Be yourself, learn all you can, and let the world know you exist.

Master closers are more than salespeople. They are the ones who keep progress and prosperity moving forward, making new ideas worth the risk, and ensuring that the windows of opportunity never shut. Masters know that when you live the way you want, that in itself is success.

Today, there are many sales books on the market that try to make the art of closing any deal complicated and basically difficult, but sales is not that complex. All sales actually is is an exchange of emotions.

Most people who study sales want to go straight to the heart of the matter and learn new closes and closing methods that will immediately make them money. That's just normal human behavior. Who wouldn't want to cut through all the peripheral information to get to what is thought to be the best part? But this is important: If a person doesn't comprehend the fundamental mechanics of sales, then the greatest one minute closes on earth won't do any good. They will be used and misused by people who don't realize their total impact, or they will be delivered in a shallow and confusing manner, which will take away the closes' intended lasting power.

In this book, I first share important knowledge I've learned throughout my life regarding master closers: how they think and believe, how customers behave and evaluate, and finally one minute closes and one minute closing procedures and how they are executed.

Before addressing the secret sales and closing lessons, I would like to say something concerning master closers. Reader, I have learned over many years and miles that salespeople in this world exist either in the "survival" mode or the "living" mode, meaning some salespeople live from draw to draw, or commission check to commission check, while others earn more than enough money to really live and enjoy life.

Master one minute closers from around the world realize they need a definite purpose in their lives that makes them want to succeed day in and day out. They understand that if someone doesn't have that need in their being, that something they are willing to sacrifice all for, then they have never really lived. So many times you hear salespeople say, "I'm going to do this," or, "I'm going to do that." Well, the truth is, "I'm agonna" never did anything. That's why master closers have a mission, and that is to be the best they can possibly be in their profession. Keep in mind, masters try to improve and ascertain new sales information all the time so they won't someday fail and despairingly fall into that ever-present and haunting "survival" mode.

It's been accepted throughout history that "you can't make a silk purse out of a sows' ear" and "you can't teach an old dog new tricks." I'm here to tell you these sayings are some of the worst lies ever penned. People can change, any time they want. Sooner or later, closers realize that it's their life, their choice, and their responsibility to be all or nothing. Master closers also appreciate that their habits—good or bad—at some point in their lives turn into their character.

Master closers are extremely competitive, and at heart, risk takers. They understand that any and all progress has resulted from people's taking unpopular positions and unvalued stands. Therefore, they are not about to surrender their sometimes controversial drive or determination to anyone. Success, to a master one minute closer, is accomplished each day he meets a new customer and convinces him or her to purchase a product that he believes in.

The master is not afraid of living on the edge, or

afraid of boundaries, knowing these limitations were created by people who couldn't see any further. The Japanese have a saying, "The nail that sticks out gets the hammer." In reality, there is no such hammer, except in people's own hand hitting themselves in the head and saying, "I'm not good enough," or, "I can't make it."

Today, in this high-tech world, there is a real need for the enthusiasm and vision of master closers. Customers subconsciously want to be around and associate with people who specialize and invest in the impossible, and master one minute closers are those people.

Reader, in all of my travels, I never discovered one single master closer who, when things were not going right, or heartache ruled a lonely night on the road, didn't stop believing in himself, and always, when no one was around, asked for help and strength in prayer.

The ABC's of international business = Always Be Closing.

—*Sir Stewart Williamson, Edinburgh, Scotland*

Note: Every company, organization, industry, and corporation in the world depends solely on its sales department to bring in money. All other company departments spend money or take money to run. So in truth, if it weren't for master one minute closers, there would be no companies.

Part II
What Master One Minute Closers Know and Understand About Themselves

I can persuade anyone, if first,
I persuade myself.

—*Sepp Nagle, Munich, Germany*

Master closers from around the world, men and women who are absolutely the best in their chosen profession, have contributed the information contained in this book.

Below is a letter that has been translated from German and was circulated throughout the sales department of a major insurance company in Europe.

The Master Closer

A master sales closer is a very complex and controversial human being. He or she is an eternal optimist, gifted with a personality that can inspire, befriend, or make enemies in only a matter of seconds. A master closer is a person who is totally convinced the future brings nothing but good fortune and fulfillment, while at the same time, failing to plan any course of action leading toward that belief. In fact, most master closers have a tendency to spend more money than they make, seemingly ignoring any financial strategies designed to ensure some feeling of security, habitually unconcerned about tomorrow or consequences. Master closers are blessed with a spirit that continually looks for worth and excellence in others, ever alert and ready to encourage, help, or advise, but curiously deaf to their own tenor, unable to forget past mistakes or troubles, silently harboring guilt and regrets. Unnecessary burdens no soul should bear. Master closers are also blessed with an overabundance of love, a pure, giving, and caring attitude all people need. Still, when the charismatic closer looks inquisitively into a mirror, what should be remembered is forgotten, erased by unexpected moments of doubt, apprehensions casting different shades of shadows on resolve, and usefulness, threatening courage itself. Master closers (it should be confessed) are fearlessly independent, living daily in a world most people could never envision, much less endure. Relying only on themselves for success, ever immersed in an atmosphere that has no boundaries, set rules, or horizons. Master closers thrive on excitement and nerve, always persistent, and perpetually living in the now, surviving on opportunities and chance, willingly risking all to perform and persuade. Master closers, in all honesty, pray. They know, honor, and cherish their source of strength. They grow and develop from torments, trials, and humility, embrace hope, defend what's right, and trust the depth and power of truth. Master closers don't wear their faith on their sleeve, but live the convictions they hold dear in deeds, words, and understanding; absolutes that radiate more compassion than a thousand hymns. Yes, the master closer is a complex and controversial soul, sometimes wise, sometimes foolish, sometimes boisterous, rebellious, unpredictable, undisciplined, behind schedule, and difficult to figure out. Not surprisingly, with an ego no objection, negative action, or obstacle can destroy, the master closer carries on. Advancing with a sureness and determination few have experienced, or dared. Also, moving and reacting with a definite certainty so passionate, so positive, any standing in the way will be changed forever. Realizing in time that without the powerful master closer, all and any progress, commerce, trade, and expressions of individuality would be tragically frozen in a stagnated society. In truth, if it weren't for the ventures, enthusiasm, and boldness of master closers, whose imagination invites unlimited possibilities, then all the endeavors of humankind would simply disappear, and the very heart of humankind would soon, without hope, accept surrender.

I sell with my heart, not predictable or scripted words.
—*Omar Boco, Johannesburg, South Africa*

FACT 1. Master closers know they are good

All professional master closers, no matter what company, organization, or industry they're in, know for a fact they are good at their job. It doesn't matter how humble they act, how delusive they seem to be, or how arrogant they are, secretly they genuinely believe there is no one in the world better than they are at selling.

True, master closers are moody and unpredictable,

seemingly changing at the drop of a hat, but in reality, within that look of chaos and restlessness, there is a well-founded and stabilizing element called ego. Because of that ego (developed through years of success), master closers keep their attitude positive, even in the bleakest of times, confidently fueled by the knowledge that "I am the best."

I fight to believe in myself, even when others have given up on me.
—*John L. Delainey, Shannon, Ireland*

FACT 2. **The two major problems master closers must overcome**

All master closers, day in and day out, have to be alert and on guard against two lax and careless habits: not holding on to their "can do" attitude and prejudging other people.

To keep an assertive attitude, master closers must simply visualize all of their victories, good days, plans, and accomplishments, not letting anyone or anything interfere with that mind-set.

Note: Before meeting with customers, most master closers seek solitude by going someplace alone, so there will be no outside situations or persons intruding on their "positive" concentration. Another thing master closers do is stay away from negative people. Such folks cannot contribute in any way whatsoever to another's heart that is set on success.

Master closers also must continually resist the temptation to prejudge other people. Nearly everyone judges everyone else before they get to know them. This, of course, is a destructive habit master closers battle against constantly, always wise to the philosophy, "People often hate everything they don't understand." Master closers train themselves to look at everyone as a special (one-of-a-kind) individual, one who has his or her own story to tell and one who through personal lessons and experience in life can (if only listened to and understood) contribute valuable knowledge not to be found anywhere else.

Again, master closers protect themselves daily from anything that could sabotage their positive attitude, and masters look for greatness in others.

Note: What we don't like about others is usually what we don't like about ourselves.

To have people care about you, you have to care about them first.
—*Robert Armstrong, London, United Kingdom*

FACT 3. For master closers, dreams are tangible

Master closers realize if you have a dream, something in your life you are willing to work for as hard as humanly possible, that dream can and will eventually become reality. There is a German saying, "You're never given a dream or a desire without the power to make it come true." This statement is fact. The want for something, if great enough and honorable enough, will in itself generate a power made up of enthusiasm and determination that can overcome any and all barriers, fears, or doubts.

There are many people in the business world who think master closers are not realists, but only dreamers, living in a world of fantasy. The master closer is a dreamer, always thinking that tomorrow will be better than today, that the next customer will buy more product than the one before, that one day, he or she will have his or her own sales team and run it better than anyone could have imagined. Yes, the master closer is a dreamer, always looking ahead and always getting solid sales results.

It should be remembered, if it weren't for dreamers and their moving force, there would be no new development in commerce. Masters know the people who succeed let their dreams, not their finances, determine their position in life. If a master closer ever stops dreaming and wanting more, that will be the day the spirit of economic hope lowers its head and dies.

I would rather dream, try, and risk all than just survive and regret.

—Bill Olsen, Dallas, Texas

FACT 4. Keep your business to yourself

Master closers keep their business to themselves, and that means both in their professional life and in their private life. Everyone has his own self to answer to. If others are curious and inquisitive, they usually have their own agenda, and it can be pretty well guaranteed that their agenda won't be beneficial to anyone but them. Master closers know through trial and error that when people ask how they are, of the people who ask, 80 percent don't care if the master closer has problems, and the other 20 percent are glad he has them. So, with that in mind, master closers simply make it a rule to say "everything's fine" when asked.

The master closer who keeps his business close to the vest will always be more successful and confident than the salesperson who lets others know his every thought or feeling, a very foolish practice that only invites gossip, rumor, and speculation, three board members of a very harmful committee.

From some people, I expect cheap shots, but I surely would not contribute the ammunition.

—Lord Esterbrook, Southhampton, United Kingdom

FACT 5. No one knows you but you

When a master closer hears someone say, "I know what's good for you," or, "I know you; I think you should do this or that," he takes it with a grain of salt, because he knows no one knows him better than he knows himself. Master closers let other people know only what they want them to know. It's their way to be independent, and keep safe their own emotions and beliefs. If a master closer discloses his strong points and weaknesses to practically everyone he talks to, he's put himself in a compromising position where others have the potential to control. For the master closer, this can only mean disaster, diminishing the power of his sales techniques, which are best presented on his own terms.

If other people think they know you and have figured you out, they can take you for granted, dismiss you, even walk all over you. The world stays curious about things and people it's not sure of, so as long as the master keeps up a mystique, he can be assured he will not be ignored or neglected.

Master closers take risks daily to follow their bliss, and reach for their destiny, while taking care to hold their cards close to their vest.

The more advice I follow, the farther I find myself from my goals.

—D. L. Rivera, Mexico City, Mexico

FACT 6. The master closer's personality is everything

The master closer knows that one's personality is strictly a state of mind, and he depends on it for survival. A master closer can accomplish and prosper without a higher education, trophies, or for that matter, good health, but never without the radiance of self. The personality one exhibits interacting with others is the key to communication. If one can't express one's thoughts and feelings in a way that causes others to listen, take interest, and understand, then all the learning and wisdom in the world are of no use.

People like others who make them feel good, who make them laugh and feel important and respected. An outgoing, friendly, diplomatic personality will do just that. To have this kind of disposition one must get into the habit of being sociable and thoughtful. It will take some time, dedication, and concentration, but again that old saying will ring true, "A person's habits do turn into his character." And that good character is both achievable and invaluable.

If I try hard enough, I can make people see me as I see myself, and I like what I see.

—Gino Musso, Rome, Italy

FACT 7. The secret of becoming great

When looking back at famous individuals in history, statements like "So-and-so was born to be a great leader" are often made. Well, those claims are often not as true as they sound. Anyone, at any time and in any place, can become a leader so charismatic and magnificent the entire world will sit up and take notice. To appreciate this concept, one must first know the basic and underlying truth that makes people great. That truth is this: People don't make themselves great; what makes people great is the cause they believe in. When a person (no matter his background or environment) has a definite objective, belief, or want he is willing to sacrifice all for, that conviction will be the catalyst for his emotions, strength, and bold actions. When someone is wholly convinced of something, the world will watch in amazement.

Success is mostly a steady repetition of the fundamentals, with a dose of risk and faith thrown in.

—*Lynn Sanford, Phoenix, Arizona*

The note below was written by a captain in the American Civil War. It was dated December 22, 1862.

Leaders

The greatest leaders are the ones who share all of their wisdom, hoping others become much greater than themselves. When people honestly know that you want more success for them than yourself, then you will have an audience whose loyalty and love is unshakable. You will have no competition.

On the other hand, if you feel superior to your audience because you know something they don't, or you boast, overlook their intelligence, or take them for granted, then you and your message will be instantly forgotten, as it rightly should be.

If I can make one person believe, then I know I can make a million others.

—*Manual Santiago, Madrid, Spain*

FACT 8. **Every bad thing that happens is good**

If a master closer hasn't experienced failure and disappointment, he doesn't have the credentials to genuinely empathize or sympathize with someone who has. Experience, as everyone knows, is an unrivaled educator, and the more one explores, inquires, learns, and dares, the more one will have the wisdom and scars to help advise and console others. If a person is afraid of getting involved with others, or going out in the world and participating, fearful he or she might get hurt in some way, that person is not really living.

Master closers use their life experiences to communicate, relate, and bond with others. So, in the world of sales, it's not surprising to see masters use their failures and heartaches to their own advantage, while at the same time caring and sharing with others as best they can.

If you want to be a great leader, then make the people around you great leaders.

—*Dell Litton, London, United Kingdom*

FACT 9. Master closers are actors

Master closers understand that if their customer is not relaxed and attentive, they will not get a sale. Customers want to feel they have a person they can confide in and share some of their personal views with. And (whether they consciously know it or not), they also want to be entertained. Knowing this, the master will intentionally wear different hats for different customers, keeping in mind one of the major "golden rules" concerning relation-ships with people: "Be sad with sad people, and happy with happy people." For example, when a master closer meets a customer who is down in the dumps about some-thing, the master will tactfully commiserate so there is a common emotion established. Then, when both parties are communicating and understand each other, the mas-ter will slowly raise the "emotional bar" and bring the customer's attitude up a few positive degrees so there is a healthier environment to present the product being sold.

Master closers are some of the greatest actors in the

world. They aren't afraid to use every backdrop and prop available to spotlight their talents, and, of course, their product.

If you are going to be magnificent, then you had better act magnificent.

—Jerry Blevins, New York, New York

FACT 10. If you want to be the best, you're already 51 percent there

Desire and determination are a lot more important than product knowledge. True, you have to know what you are talking about concerning the product, but if one doesn't have that burning dedication to be the best, to outperform everyone else, product facts might as well be delivered by a stand-in robot. As stated before, master closers are very competitive and highly motivated. They are the kind of individuals who always want, and will lead any sales team that's put together. When a closer truly wants to be a top producer, he is already over 51 percent of the way toward that goal of being the best. The proven universal secret here is to stay focused, believe in yourself, and never, never give up.

The people who succeed in life are the ones who don't give in to hardships or to others' interference. The master is no different, and he acknowledges that the only true enemy with the power to stop him from becoming the best is himself. He embraces the Chinese saying, "When there is no real enemy within me, then any enemy that is found outside will not ever hurt me." He trusts in his talents while continually focusing on his wants, knowing diversion and compliancy could make all desires fall out of reach.

You will never find your rightful place in life until you first courageously take steps, and go out and search for it.

—*Marco Salvini, Milan, Italy*

FACT 11. No master closer has all the answers

Every master closer in the world admits he can learn something new from anyone, at any time. A master closer will always keep his mind open to other opinions and different closing ideas that might make him a better closer or increase his closing percentage. The saying, "The more I know, the more I know I know nothing," is very truthful. Therefore, eagerness to ask questions and investigate anything that might help him keep on top of the selling profession is an essential asset. The day the master closer stops learning, listening, and asking questions is the very day the world passes him by.

In sales, all things, at some point in time, have to change. So, in truth, all things, at some point in time, can stay the same.

—*Hidio Enocie, Tokyo, Japan*

FACT 12. Negative people are destructive

The biggest menace any master closer can come across is pessimistic people. These sad people are poison, and to make matters worse, many times they are upset and cynical about things they don't fully understand. Unfortunately, most people who are negative want to believe any and all bad news they have been fed. Master closers have learned through the years to simply ignore such people. Master closers don't let discouraging people drag them down or make them feel bad or guilty. The master, when encountering a pessimistic personality, is pleasant and tactfully walks away. Negative people can be a danger to progress, not to mention a bitter affront to faith.

A mean-spirited whisper can be heard around the world.

—Jon Dinsman, Kansas City, Missouri

FACT 13. Master closers can and do start over

A German monk named Thomas à Kempis once said, "Man judges you by your actions, but God judges you by your intentions." Now, that is a wonderful thought that should be kept close. Unfortunately, many people prejudge and misjudge master closers and their good intentions, which can taint the sales office environment. Too often, master closers will find fellow salespeople, or even some sales managers, out to sabotage their production, because of their high sales percentages. When circumstances like this arise, the master has three options: The first is to quit and move to a new job; the second is to stay and fight; the third is to compromise. In most every case, the master closer will leave, feeling that any continuation of anxieties or hostilities is not worth the energy. The master realizes from his experiences that trying to hang on and persevere is most likely an unhealthy choice that will take a great toll not only on him, but on the company as well. If and when a master closer decides to leave his job, he will do some soul searching and attitude adjusting, and will look forward with vigor to a new start, considering the past only as a lesson well learned.

The master closer will never in a million years live his life below his abilities. He will change, if necessary, by taking one step at a time and by using his past accomplishments as tools, ever determined to find the right venue for his God-given talents.

Reader, years ago someone asked a master closer why he was leaving his sales position, and he gave an unforgettable answer: "I'm not sure where I'm going, but I'm sure I can't get there from here."

I moved, regrouped, rejuvenated myself, and strengthened myself, all the while keeping in mind who I was and what I wanted to accomplish in life, and in no time at all, I was back on top of the world.

—*Randel M. Roberts, Melbourne, Australia*

FACT 14. **Three words that kill**

Out of the tens of thousands of words in the English language, the three words used the most are "I," "me," and "my." Master closers purposely stay away from these three subliminal sales destroyers. Customers instinctively want to hear their name spoken before any "I," "me," and "my."

The customer doesn't need the closer in order to make a living. Instead, the closer needs the customer in order to make a living, so it is very important that the master take the emphasis off his presence and focus solely on the customer. One of the most noticeable and direct ways of doing that is to stop using, or a least cut down on using, the words "I," "me," and "my," and to replace them with words such as "us," "we," "our," "yours," "you," and so on. This shows consideration and attention to the customer. It will take time to break the habit of using these sales-killing pronouns, but with practice, "I," "me," and "my" will soon disappear from your conversation, and it can be guaranteed, sales will increase.

In life, good judgment usually comes from past experiences. Unfortunately, most past experiences come from bad judgment.

—*Gary Mathews, London, United Kingdom*

FACT 15. Master closers sell only what they believe in

One of the worst things a closer can do, besides lie to his customer, is try to sell a product he doesn't believe in, or own himself. Customers are not feebleminded; they can sense something isn't right when a salesman who privately doubts his product is giving a sales presentation, and his expected level of energy and enthusiasm seems to be absent. This obvious lack of fervor will, of course, throw up red flags, creating doubts in the customer that will make him feel uneasy, and in the final analysis, decide not to purchase. There is nothing that will motivate and embolden a closer more than knowing he is selling the best product available, at the best price on the market.

It's this kind of security that will make any closer, if he's worth his salt, energetic, fascinating, and deadly. Customers cannot resist any positive force that is grounded in truth and sincerity. They will willingly get caught up in the presentation excitement and buy, if, of course, finances aren't the problem.

Now, if a master closer is selling a product and, at some point, discovers the product is a scam, or not as advertised, the master will simply quit his job and walk away. He knows there will always be opportunities for good closers, and to try selling something just for the commission not only weakens him over the long run, but steals away pieces of self-respect with every check he receives. Customers can see in the closer's eyes and in the aura surrounding him that he isn't completely convinced he's presenting the very best to his patrons.

Truthfully, I can only sell as good as my product is.

—*W. Frank Schuler, Frankfurt, Germany*

FACT 16. Twenty percent, the law of nature

If a closer can't consistently sell at least one out of five customers (20 percent), he's not a closer. Even in the law of nature, 20 percent is the common denominator. For instance, when a big cat in the jungle, let's say a tiger, goes out to hunt, the cat will only make one kill out of five attempts. If a farmer plants five seeds of corn, only one will germinate. Twenty percent is the magic number in nature, and it should be the magic number in human communication. All master closers need a true rule of measure by which to evaluate their performance and the "20 percent law" is the best.

Note: If a master closer doesn't have around 10 percent of his sales cancel, then he is not selling at his full potential. A true master closer knows his job is theoretically to sell every customer he talks to, and if he is doing the job expected of him, he will have people who get wrapped up in the "sales" moment and purchase, only to rescind after they take a few steps back and realize what they have done, or committed themselves to. Now, this cancellation phenomenon is not something bad, or something to be ashamed of, but a simple reminder of common human behavior, proving the master closer is doing his job by doing what he does best; trying to sell everyone he talks to.

Without a tough, powerful, and defensive customer, a master closer would never know how tough, powerful, and good he is.

—*Tony Angelli, Rome, Italy*

FACT 17. Master closers don't cheat people

The true master closer knows that sales practices bordering on activities that could be illegal often lead nowhere and are rewarded with regrets or destruction. Honesty is, and always will be, the fundamental pillar a master closer stands on to soundly and boldly present his product. This pillar of integrity gives the master the courage and fortitude to face and overcome any obstacle or objection the most difficult customer can come up with. Without the alliance of truth, master closers wouldn't and couldn't sell the high percentage of customers they do.

Respect customers, befriend customers, and tell the truth with passion, and you will have a very prosperous selling life, one in which you can be happy and don't have to look over your shoulder everywhere you go.

When you put another person first, you will never be last.

—*Janelle Lindsey, Tulsa, Oklahoma*

FACT 18. **Dress the way you feel comfortable**

Master closers will dress the way they want. Even if the company they work for has a dress code, the closer will find a way to show his individuality. This is not to be interpreted as a rebellious statement, but just part of a master closer's nature.

The two sayings, "First impressions are lasting impressions," and, "Always dress better than your customer," don't hold up as often as people think. Master closers believe, and in most cases it's true, that no matter what they wear, their personality and charisma will overshadow their apparel. It can be guaranteed, if the master has been around long enough, he knows what works for him and what doesn't.

Now, as far as jewelry goes (and this pertains to both men and women closers), if the master wears a lot of rings, bracelets, or chains, it is important, even though it seems like a small matter, to explain to the customer what the jewelry represents. For instance, the closer could tell the customer, if it applies, that the ring he is wearing was his grandfather's, or the chain was a wedding present, and so on, so the customer understands the meaning of the glitter. If this subject is not addressed head-on, the customer will think to himself that the closer is too self-indulgent, "high and mighty," or self-absorbed, which could cause unnecessary feeling of animosity, thus making the sale that much more difficult.

One more time, because this is important: If excessive jewelry is not explained to the customer, then that one skipped-over subject could very well bring up questions and doubts on the customers' part, creating a curiousness the customer will keep inside and speculate about on his own. The customer could very well develop an attitude of resentment that would silently override and drown out the closer's total sales presentation, thus making the sale almost impossible.

The master closer never forgets the well-known rule "keep it simple," and that includes not only the closer's verbiage, but also wardrobe and accessories.

Humility has no enemies.

—*Natami Kamochi, Tokyo, Japan*

FACT 19. Master closers control their jobs

Master closers know from experience that if they don't control their job and schedules, their work will control them, thus creating an environment in which the closer finds himself running around in circles and wasting a lot of valuable time. The commonsense thing to remember is to keep a schedule that is comfortable. That way, a closer doesn't rush through customers, talk to a lot of people, and wind up selling nothing. Most master closers keep a schedule and goal of ninety days at a time. In other words, they work hard for ninety days, relax for five days, then work another ninety days and relax for another five days. If a closer works diligently for three ninety-day periods of time, on the fourth ninety-day period, he will have enough money to take off and vacation. Almost all master closers around the world work only nine months out of the year. They will not, under any circumstances, be chained to their job.

The master closer is very capricious and self-ruling. If he feels his office is pressuring him into a corner, or threatening his maneuverability, he will move on, finding an organization where he feels he can breathe and be himself.

I work as hard as I want, play as hard as I want, and never let one interfere with the other.

—*Jerry Sikes, Sydney, Australia*

FACT 20. The secret of one's destiny

Every professional closer in the world has one deep-seated desire he lives with day and night, and that is to be independently wealthy. Master closers know they have the talent and fortitude to make this dream come true, but unforeseen circumstances keep arising, causing this dream to seemingly slip further away with each passing year. That is one of the reasons master closers are so restless, and eager to find the right company or opportunity to settle down with and accumulate enough money to start their own company or sales team, which in turn will reward them with the capital needed to see their dream realized.

The worst thing that can happen to a master closer is to start doubting and forgetting his true goals in life, and become complacent, slowly giving up and giving in while accepting the belief that a decent commission check is good enough. This kind of defeatist attitude is an insult to any master closer who is blessed with so many gifts and people skills. Master closers are meant to live their dreams. They are meant to be successful, and they are meant to touch the hearts of other, making this (in the long run) a better world.

The following excerpt is from a letter written to a young man fifty years ago by his father, who was one of the leading bankers in Santiago, Chile. This note on destiny has been translated from Spanish.

The Secret of Destiny

Your destiny is discovered and revealed through your dreams and beliefs that reinforce your desire to act and follow your passion. Every day of your life, you are reminded, by your thoughts, of the purpose of your life. The very reason for your existence and the responsibility you are entrusted with. In truth, you only have an obligation to listen to yourself and do what you want, while respecting others. The secret of your destiny is forged from the talents and wisdom you possess, steadily interwoven and coupled with experience that, over time, opens its doors of possibility and discloses the road you are to follow toward prosperity. Every person lives for a purpose, but far too many don't follow their appointed path. They don't understand or disregard their potential. They mock their talents by taking them for granted, and ignore the designed gifts from God, which are given freely to accomplish, and positively affect both earth and man.

The master closer requires freedom and independence to seek his own fate. He needs strength and determination to procure his destiny, without the heavy weights of suspicion, skepticism, or jealousy from others, petty abuses that can hold a person captive, or redirect his ambitions. Masters know that when a person bows to the whims and wants of another, forgetting self, that person's special persona will eventually be lost, slowly disappearing into shadows of sorrow, shadows that hide the smallest rays of hope.

The lost closer seeks the lost, and the prosperous closer seeks the prosperous, while the closer who stands alone is sought by both.

—*William Stewart, Glasgow, Scotland*

This concludes Part II of the book. The next subjects to be discussed are important facts master closers have found over the years concerning customers. Even in this high-tech age of electronic and nano-fiberoptic wonder, people skills will always be needed. It doesn't matter if communication is done via computers, satellite phones, or any other method, closers need to know human nature. They need to understand why people behave a certain way and how they think. Sales will always be a profession based on psychology, and psychology is simply the science of people.

The mean and unjust salesperson will be talked about forever, but the kind and just master closer will be remembered forever.

—Linda Rollow, Denver, Colorado

Part III
What Master One Minute Closers Know and Understand About Customers

Reason directs the customers' actions, while emotions control the customers' actions.

—*George Westbrook, Memphis, Tennessee*

I n the next few pages, master one minute closers reveal what they have learned about customers, worldwide. The knowledge and conclusions that follow come from years of experience. The reader should keep in mind that everything written in this book comes from the wisdom of the very best one minute closers on earth.

If you truly know and understand yourself, then you can control your world, but if you listen, know, and understand others, you can control the whole world.

—*Evelyn Scott, Oxford, United Kingdom*

FACT 1. Customers are not complicated

Everyone in the world is a customer several times a day, day in, day out, and year after year. All people, no matter their station in life, origin, country, or religion, turn into customers, with all the trappings and thoughts of a customer, the second they go out to shop or exchange ideas and beliefs with others. When a person puts himself into the role of a customer, all the rules change in favor of the master closer because the master is an expert when it comes to one-on-one relationships.

All people, when in the mode of a customer, basically behave and think the same. True, their excuses and stories will be different to some degree, but their primary demeanor and overall philosophy will rarely change. The master closer has learned a very valuable lesson concerning customers over the years, and that is that customers are relatively simple. Now, this does not mean customers are simple-minded; quite the contrary. It means customers fundamentally want four clear conditions when they buy a product. One, they don't want to be lied to or cheated, two, they want a good and fair price, three, they want a sound and reliable product, and four, they want a product they can be proud of. If a master closer can satisfy all four of these conditions, while at the same time befriending the customer and making the customer feel untroubled, a sale will be made.

Customers want to have peace of mind during the sales presentation, and the master creates this comfortable atmosphere by listening to his customers with interest and by making the customers feel important, giving them a true sense of value, which reinforces their self-confidence. Customers want and like to buy things if money isn't the issue. Again, customers are not as complicated and complex as they might seem.

Always treat little people like they are important, and treat important people with respect.

—*Unknown*

FACT 2. It's difficult to dislike people who like you

The master closer depends heavily on this one important secret concerning human nature. "There is not a person in the world who can dislike someone who likes him or makes him laugh." Now, a person might not like another person's actions, habits, or manner, but to dislike someone who genuinely exhibits friendship is almost impossible. This is a basic law of human behavior the master uses to full advantage. For example, he will intentionally find something he likes about his customer and then make a sincere and positive comment on that something.

Note: Customers know what's good about themselves, and what's not so good, so the closer had better be honest when he makes his observation or his compliment could be misconstrued as disingenuous or as cheap flattery.

Now, when the closer makes a friendly statement, one that moves the customer to feel valued and proud, the customer will automatically, without any reservations, like the closer. And if the customer likes the closer, he will listen to the closer, and if he listens to the closer, he'll believe the closer, and if he believes the closer, and he can afford the product, he'll buy. It's as simple as that.

The way a customer dresses usually reflects his personality, because most people won't wear something they are not proud of.

—*Carl Stikes, Pretoria, South Africa*

<u>FACT 3.</u> Happy customers versus unhappy customers

This is a fact most salespeople don't realize, but all master closers do. If a master sells a customer, and that customer is happy, on average, the satisfied customer will tell only two or three other people about the experience. If a closer makes the customer unhappy, or upsets the customer in any way, the disgruntled customer will, on average, tell eight to ten people. This, of course, doesn't benefit anyone. No matter how the closer leaves his customer, meaning sale or no sale, he makes sure the customer feels he was treated fairly and has found a new friend. The master never lets a customer go who is annoyed or angry. He will always take the time to calm the customer down, if need be, and makes the customer aware he is welcome back at any time. If a closer thinks it's cute or good for his ego to "burn" a customer, he's a fool.

Note: Many years ago, there was a major product manufacturer that would sell one defective product for every nine good products sold. Now, this one-to-ten ratio was intentional, so the customer who bought the defective product would come back to the company, complaining and upset. When this occurred, the sales director would apologize profusely, immediately replace the bad product with a good product, and tell the customer that from now on, he alone would be the person to call if anything was needed, thus cutting through any red tape. The sales director would also give the troubled customer a few extras, pens, calendar, hat, etc., to make him feel special. Remember, reader, this whole exercise was planned and calculated by the company, because the sales division of that company knew if an unhappy customer was well taken care of and treated like a VIP after he found his product was defective, or not what he expected, that once-disheartened customer would go out and be a great representative and cheerleader for the company, bringing in more new customers at a cost far less than the company had previously spent on advertising. Of course, this is not the way to do business, but at the time, the company's practice of making unhappy customers happy and using the satisfied VIP customer to generate new customers worked wonders.

The greatest master closers always make friends, even when traveling a road leading into the unknown.

—*Juan Garcia, Marbella, Spain*

FACT 4. Six major reasons customers don't buy

When all is said and done, there are still only six basic excuses customers have for not purchasing, and they are:

1. The customer doesn't understand what the closer is talking about. This problem is usually caused by the closer's going into too much detail and confusing the customer. Or the closer himself doesn't understand the product and instead of admitting he doesn't have all the answers, or making it a simple, to-the-point sales presentation, keeps talking in circles. Either way, if the customer doesn't buy because of this kind of situation, it is the closer's fault alone.

2. The customer just doesn't care for the closer. If this is the case, and there could be a hundred reasons why the closer and the customer don't get along, the sale is lost. The point is, if the customer dislikes a salesperson, he's sure not going to do business with the salesperson, and that can be guaranteed.

3. The customer doesn't believe what the closer is saying, either about himself, or about the company he represents, or about the product. Again, if the closer finds himself in this kind of predicament, he can only get angry with one person, and that is himself.

4. The customer just does not like the product they're being shown, or doesn't like the company that makes it. In a case like this, the closer will present another product to suit the customer's needs, if possible, or, keeping the atmosphere of politeness and trust intact, let the customer go. Even though a sale wasn't made, the master closer will always take the higher

road by being gracious and professional, while looking forward to his next customer.

5. The customer is afraid to make a decision without the approval of someone he trusts, afraid to make a commitment, or worried he may not be able to afford the product. This is where the master closer earns his commission. To help the customer overcome his indecision, he props up the customer's self-confidence and reassures the customer he is doing the right thing. The master steadily reinforces the customer's decision to purchase with positive and solid statements before and after the sale is made. Remember, in this type of situation, the closer must get the customer sold on himself, and work on his ego, building up his courage. If these two sales exercises are not used, there will be no sale.

6. The customer simply doesn't have the money. He just can't afford the product. When the closer faces this condition, the only thing he can do is give the customer some information about the product and, as politely as necessary, let him go. Remember, never degrade or humiliate someone who honestly doesn't have the financial wherewithal to purchase. Treat these customers with the same respect as someone who buys. It's the only right thing to do.

Note: In Part VII of this book, overcoming certain conditions and objections will be explained in detail.

Closers can learn a lot from customers who view the world differently than they do.

—*Randy Singelton, Windsor, Canada*

FACT 5. Treat every customer like a millionaire

Thirty years ago in Sweden, a team of international scientists attached electronic monitors to the heads of volunteer patients and recorded brain waves that showed how many thoughts a human being had during a twenty-four-hour period. This experiment was then carried out over the next ten years in twenty different countries. What the Swedish doctors and scientists found was significant. They discovered the average person, no matter where he came from or who he was, had about ninety-seven thousand thoughts during the hours he was awake. Using percentages based on certified math ratio findings, the scientists ascertained that out of the ninety-seven thousand thoughts, at least one of those thoughts, if pursued and cultivated, would be worth one million dollars. Understanding this, the master closer knows that every customer he talks to has the potential to be a multimillionaire, so with that in mind, the master treats all of his customers as if they were millionaires, thus increasing his sales percentage due to his positive and respectful attitude. The lesson here is simple. If you treat people like they are worth a million dollars, the chances are very great that they'll do business with you! Customers like to think they're special, and the master closer won't let them down.

If I get my customer sold on little things, then I know I can sell him on bigger things later.

— *Ivan Javick, Warsaw, Poland*

<u>FACT 6.</u> A customer's watch and cell phone tell all

Believe it or not, a customer's wristwatch or cell phone tells the master closer many things about his character. Remember, people don't wear or use something they are ashamed of. When talking about watches, there will always be a few exceptions. For example, folks who work in the construction business need a sturdy and reliable watch, while registered nurses require watches that have a second hand on them. In this study of watches and customers in general, the following observations usually give the master closer a pretty good thumbnail sketch of his customer's personality. Again, there will always be cases where these "watch rules" don't apply, but in most circumstances, the customer's wristwatch tells all. To start, let's say the master closer has an elderly couple for customers and the gentleman is wearing a simple watch with large numerals and a leather band. Chances are pretty good this customer is conservative, needs the large numerals because of poor eyesight, and has a lot of money in the bank. Or let's say the closer's customer is a young man, wearing a fake, gold watch. Well, it's probably safe to label this person a wannabe, who is wearing a "copycat," or knockoff watch because he can't afford a real gold watch. The master closer knows to treat a customer as if he's truly wealthy, and this type of wannabe customer will trap himself every time, because of his ego, and purchase the closer's product. If a closer has a customer wearing a designer watch, this person might be an individualist who will buy what he wants and doesn't care what others think. If a customer is wearing a watch that has a lot of bells and whistles on it, it is probable that he will be an eager buyer. Now, if a customer is wearing a real gold watch or a gold tank watch with a genuine reptile strap, chances are this customer can afford the product. If the customer isn't wearing a wristwatch, ask the customer why, and on cue, the customer will explain and tell the master closer more about himself than he intended.

As for cell phones, the closer can tell a great deal about the personality of his customer by the type of phone he uses. If the customer's phone has a lot of different functions, and is fairly expensive, the customer probably has money. If the cell phone is inexpensive, the customer has some money. If the customer has a full-service communication device, with all the latest high-tech capabilities, the closer will ask the customer for a demonstration. This builds up the ego of the customer, making him that much easier to sell.

Note: Customers with big egos always put themselves in a corner when dealing with a master closer.

Everyone is a masterpiece if others would just take the time to look.

—*William Santiago, Pueblo, Mexico*

FACT 7. All unique characters buy

Now, this is an odd statement, but it's true. All people who are eccentric and unique in character buy. When a master closer meets a unique or somewhat controversial person, the master will go along with his antics and logic to some degree, but never lose control. The master will listen intently to this customer's stories and show appreciation for what he is saying. Any customer who is or acts out of the ordinary will purchase as long as the master closer appears entertained and spellbound by the customer's exploits and personality. The main lesson here is to treat every customer as if he is the most unique and interesting people in the world. Give all customers the attention and courtesy they desire. Be humble and entertaining, making each individual customer feel wanted and needed. If these attentions are felt, and are interpreted by the customer as sincere, there will be a sale made.

Never laugh at another mans' scars, because you were not there for the wounds.

—*Unknown*

FACT 8. Most customers are risk takers

A lot of salespeople don't realize this, but most customers are willing to take risks. This is because every time a customer steps into a sales office, an environment he is unfamiliar with, and is somewhat poised to meet a closer he has never met, and is prepared to be either romanced or grilled, that customer, in plain old words, is a risk taker. It can be guaranteed that the master will use the customer's bravery and curiosity to his advantage. For example, if the customer hesitates about purchasing the closer's product, or tries to rely on some unconvincing excuse for not buying, the master closer can remind him of his positive qualities, his self-confidence, and his courage to make decisions.

Some customers are afraid to believe, because they are scared that what they want to believe in so deeply might not be true.

—*Francisco Coelmenaris, Madrid, Spain*

The customer's soul is threefold; first spirit, then reason, then desire. If all are satisfied, all is done.

—*Ian Armon, Tel Aviv, Israel*

FACT 9. The Magic Combination: 7 – 35 – 58

Master closers succeed by understanding the following very important sales fact. After a sale is made, or not made, the customer will remember only three major things about the closer himself. If the customer's total recollection of the experience is 100 percent, it breaks down the following way: 7 percent of what the average customer will remember, out of the closer's total sales presentation, involves what was said. What the customer remembers next about the closer is his tone of voice, and that made a 35 percent impact. What the customer remembers most about the closer, accounting for 58 percent of his recollection, was the closer's facial expressions. Out of the whole time the closer spent with the customer, including everything that was said and done, what the customer remembers most was the facial narration presented by the closer. Many times a sincere smile will do more good than a thousand words. Customers want to know their closer genuinely cares about them, and a certain "look" the closer gives the customer at the right time and place might be just enough of a nudge to close the deal.

Give customers the chance to feel important. If you do so, customers will act and behave as if they are important.

—*Dan Litten, New York, New York*

FACT 10. Customers Lie

This might not be politically correct to write, but since this is my final sales book, why not tell all?

Most, if not all, customers lie to the master closer sometime during the sales presentation. That's just the way it is. Customers lie and tell stories for many different reasons. Most of the reasons are ridiculous, and senseless, while others are protective barriers intended and designed to avoid embarrassment or some awkward situation. Whatever the case may be, customers are prone to fib every now and then.

Every time a master closer catches his customer in a lie, it only proves to the closer that he's either getting close to the truth or pushing hard enough to make the customer feel uneasy concerning some topic or subject being discussed. The master closer will use his gifts of persuasion to tactfully put the customer into a psychological position where the truth will come out sooner or later.

Note: In Part VII of this book, closing customers and "psychological positioning" will be examined and explained in detail.

Before meeting with a master closer, most customers have a game plan. They have worked out a secret strategy purposely drafted to fend off any aggressive closer or protect against emotions and impulsive buying decisions. Fortunately, these customer game plans are like a five-piece puzzle and are not difficult for the master closer to figure out as he evaluates the situation, identifies any problems, counters all objections, and closes the deal. No customers will ever arrive at a sales office with a game plan as complicated as a jigsaw puzzle. If they do, they will most likely get confused themselves and wind up buying.

Note: The following information comes from the Federal Bureau of Investigation and Scotland Yard, United Kingdom. It is a general "rule" used by law enforcement personnel to tell if a person is lying or not when asked a question. This rule, which has been proven to be accurate 95 percent of the time, is as follows: When someone asks another person a question and the person who was asked the question looks to the left and up, that person is trying to remember, which means that person is telling the truth. When the person who was asked the question looks to the right and up, he or she is trying to construct or make up an answer, which of course, means that person is lying. The right side of the human brain is the area in which recollection and memories are stored. This side of the brain controls the left side of the body, including the left eye, whereas the left side of the brain is the area where imagination and creativeness take place. This side of the brain controls the right side of the body, including the right eye. So, again, if a customer, when asked a question, looks to the left, he is telling the truth, and if he looks to the right, he is lying.

Don't ever confuse the customer with too many facts.

—*Unknown*

FACT 11. Make the customer thirsty

This is a simple lesson that master closers have learned at some point in their professional lives. It's very basic, but important. The following story, which helps illustrate "sales wisdom," originated in Mexico. One day, years ago, a young and excited salesman ran into his sales managers' office and said, "Remember that story you told me about taking control and leading the horse to water, then making him drink? Well, I've done that with my customer. I've led the horse to water, but I can't make him drink." The old sales manager looks up at the young salesman and says, "No, no, you've got the story all wrong. I didn't say lead the horse to water and make him drink, what I said was, lead the horse to water, but just make him thirsty, then he'll get the drink on his own." This is what master closers do with customers; they make them thirsty for their product. That way, it's a lot easier to get a sale than trying to make a hard push at the very end of the sales presentation.

Masters put their customers into the picture from the very first time they meet them. All during the sales presentation, the closer is building up the product and explaining how beneficial the product would be for the customer, and how proud the customer would feel owning the product. The closer is constantly bonding the product with the customer's personality and ego, making the customer feel attached to and comfortable with the product.

Note: When a customer wants something badly enough, he could decide to buy at any time during the sales presentation, if only asked by the closer. The master has to always be prepared to write up the sale the second the customer's emotions and excitement level are high enough.

Note: The customer's emotional and excitement level, plus the "right timing," will be discussed in detail in Part VII of this book.

Master closers are professionals who can sell anyone at any time, and it sure helps when the customer is biting at the bit, and thirsty.

Today many salespeople think getting too familiar with customers, laughing and crying with them, is just too old school. But emotions play a major role in any sales promotion or presentation. It doesn't matter how technologically sophisticated the human race gets, people will always need the company and comfort of other people. Master closers must be skilled at sensing the sentiments and passions of people even before words are spoken. They recognize when customers have concerns and fears, and are always on the lookout for any telltale sign that unlocks the door to someone's feelings.

Too old school? This author thinks not. There are too many people in the world who have only hope to hang on to. The master closer knows to never deprive someone of his hope because it may be the last thing he has. Customers will purchase a product if that product helps them accomplish something, or advances them closer to their dreams, and hope is the key factor that makes people want to act and take risks. Many customers depend on hope and its power because it gives them the incentive to become the person they want to be. Hope is a very compelling and persuasive gift master closers rely on, and use, always aware of its delicacy.

Hope makes people stand up more than they fall.

—*Barbara Simms, San Francisco, California*

FACT 12. Closers customers don't respect

Customers are many things, but few are stupid. And they will start grading their closer the second they are introduced. Customers are often suspicious that closers are not always as nice and friendly as they appear. They realize the closer is out to make a sale and that he has a dozen tricks up his sleeve to help make that happen. Customers can spot, in no time, a closer who is putting on airs, or one who is not truly sincere. Customers can usually tell when a closer doesn't care about them or the product, or is lying, because the closer's sales passion, an energy that should be all-consuming, is absent.

Note: When a closer is "laid back," or acting as though he's not interested in selling his product, that could very well be a strategic technique. In this section (Fact 12), we're only discussing the customer's impressions of a closer, nothing else.

Customers know, and don't respect, a phony smile or handshake. They can tell if a closer is nervous or unsure of himself, and they notice how other people treat and act toward a closer. Customers can get very angry and upset when they think they are being ignored, taken for granted, or made a fool of. Customers can be upset by and don't respect an overly nonchalant attitude.

Customers, without exception, want to be treated as if they are the most influential and successful people the closer has talked to in a long time, and they won't tolerate or put up with any closer who treats them differently. Customers will go out of their way to purchase a product they want from a closer they like, before buying from someone they don't care for.

If I talk continually for thirty-five minutes, my customer loses interest. If I continue to talk uninterrupted for more than an hour, my customer falls asleep.

—*Don Shofner, Tampa, Florida*

FACT 13. Customers want to trust master closers

There is nothing customers want more than to do business with a closer they can believe and depend on, someone they can recommend to their friends wholeheartedly. Customers want a closer who is bold in his convictions, is patient under pressure, and can reason honestly. They want a closer who will fight for their position and get things taken care of if the product has, or develops, some problem. Customers will not buy from a salesperson who won't look them straight in the eye. If a customer feels uncomfortable with or around a closer, for whatever reason, or suspects the closer isn't some-one he wants to disclose his personal finances to, then all is lost. Customers want to be treated with dignity and expect the closer to inform and educate them truthfully on the product. If the customer thinks, for one minute, that the closer is uninformed, is behind the times, or lacks good manners, there will be no sale. Customers want closers they can communicate with easily and can count on for fairness and excellent service.

People will buy you, because you first bought them.

—*Demarco Avanti, Lake Como, Italy*

FACT 14. The professions and business customers

The following is a breakdown of the general thinking patterns and habits unique to certain types of custom-ers. Of course, it's important to note that I'm generaliz-ing. Nevertheless, these statements apply to nearly all of my experiences, and, I think, will help the closer make more effective sales presentations when dealing with customers in these categories.

1. Accountants

Accountants are often naturally skeptical and conser-vative in their thinking. They have to study all the financial aspects of a product, or service, before buying. Accoun-tants can often be closed using a negative presentation, with steady intimidating pressure applied. The closer should always let the accountant think he is in control. This customer will more times than not trap himself.

2. Airline pilots

Pilots are decision makers and therefore most are individual-minded, with a high degree of professional pride. They are often good-natured, personable, and open-minded, as well as logical and optimistic. Pilots are big buyers all the way. They can be closed by building up their egos and showing respect for their profession. An enthusiastic sales presentation is a must to get pilots properly motivated to buy.

3. Artists

Artists tend to see things in a different light than the average customer. They can be both optimistic and pessimistic in their outlook, depending on their mood. They tend to approach your product or service in a casual manner. Artists can be closed by demonstrating the advantages of owning the product or service. Steady, clear, hard-hitting pressure is often needed in your presentation to ensure that they really respond to your pitch.

4. Bankers

Like accountants, bankers can be conservative and generally skeptical. Because they are thinkers and analyzers, not excitable buyers, it is likely they will study and pick a product apart with intensity. They often don't like pressure and want everything in a presentation to be organized. Bankers can be closed by a negative sales presentation it if is given with a confident air of professionalism. Low-key pressure can be successfully used with a casual and well-thought-out close.

5. Barbers/stylists

Hairdressers are often independent and know how to make a decision; they can be creative and generally possess an optimistic outlook. They are artists to a degree and will have similar characteristics, except that they may be more practical, as they often own their own businesses. Hairdressers can be closed with a solid, logical, positive sales presentation. The keys are enthusiasm and ownership advantage.

6. Bartenders and club owners

Bartenders and club owners are independent thinkers who know how to make a decision. They are good buyers and will often make quick buying decisions. Because of their independent streak, they know what they want and go after it. They are personable, understanding, and self-motivated. They are good for referrals.

They can be closed by using a positive, enthusiastic sales presentation showing plenty of excitement.

7. Coaches

Coaches can make buying decisions, but they have to be led because sometimes they can feel out of place when not around the team, where they are leaders. They are not as self-motivated as you might expect. They want a good deal and don't worry too much about details. Coaches can best be closed by working on their ego and pride. A positive, pressure presentation should be used. The closer should attempt to get this customer to talk about his profession—usually one he enjoys immensely. You should try to get friendly and comfortable with this customer before putting on the close.

8. High-tech/computer industry professionals

In general, people in these professions are not excitable and must be guided into a buying decision. Have all your facts and figures handy and you can dazzle them with information most other customers couldn't care less about. Don't try to be too chatty or you may overwhelm them. They can usually be sold with a pressure close using steady intimidation. They often have to be pushed into the sale. To accomplish this, the closer should always first build their confidence up and try to make them feel special, before closing.

9. Construction industry personnel

People in the construction business are often money-oriented and will buy after being shown the advantages of the product. They are a positive and quick decision-making group. They will not require great detail on a product, but want to be sure it is sound. They are personable and will take a chance. People in construction are serious buyers all the way. They can be closed by showing logical financial advantage and excitement concerning the product. A positive, aggressive sales presentation should be used. The closer should allow these customers to have some control. They respond especially well when you focus on the ownership benefits of your product or service.

10. Dentists

Most dentists do not have the air of importance that many physicians have, but they are still thinkers and analyzers, not impulse buyers. They want logic and facts concerning the presentation and the product. They are independent and will make a decision if the product is presented in a professional manner. They can be closed with facts and a very personable sales presentation. Remember, they are also in a people business and will respond to the closer if he opens up a little. Enthusiasm and manners are a must to close this type of professional client.

11. Electricians, carpenters, plumbers, and so on

They are buyers, and they will react on impulse if excited about a product. They work hard, make good money, and want to spend it. They are very open-minded and will ask only basic buying questions. They are not usually detail people; they just want the satisfaction of knowing they got a good deal. They are good referral customers. They can be closed with a positive, enthusiastic sales presentation. Use friendship and some leadership when selling them. Showmanship will also contribute to closing this sale.

12. Engineers

Engineers are obviously numbers people. They want to examine and analyze everything. They are careful thinkers and sometimes procrastinators. They are not impulse buyers and can be difficult to motivate. They think logically and reason with little emotion. Engineers can be closed by a negative presentation using logic and facts. They should think they are in control and be allowed to direct the conversation, especially into areas where they have expertise. They will often trap themselves, if given enough time and maneuvered properly by the closer.

13. Entertainers

Entertainers are often optimistic and aggressive. They can be very independent and stubborn in their decision-making, but are easily persuaded to buy if motivated. They can be moody and need some leadership. Work gently on their egos. They are best closed with a sales presentation that is full of excitement and enthusiasm. The closer should go out of his way to make this customer feel important and respected, something the customer is very used to and, in most cases, expects.

14. Entrepreneurs

Entrepreneurs can lead you through the sales presentation if you aren't careful. They are self-motivated, aggressive, and optimistic. They are also unusually open-minded and think well on their feet. They can and will make a buying decision on the spot. These people know how to handle themselves and know what they like, so a soft sell is a must. Entrepreneurs can be closed by showing admiration and respect for their successes. The closer should give a positive, enthusiastic sales presentation while all the time working on their egos. Don't start boring these customers or you will quickly be history, as they'll move on to another source for your product or service. Remember that they are also great at sales or they wouldn't be successful entrepreneurs—so don't ever underestimate them.

15. Executives

Believe it or not, executives often need leadership when buying for themselves. They are self-motivated and optimistic but need some gentle guidance. They want a good deal and like to think they made the decision themselves concerning a product they are buying. They can be sold all the way if their egos are properly massaged. The closer should show professionalism and logic, treating the executive as if he were the owner of his company instead of just a pencil-pushing manager. Work on this customer's ego and ability to make a decision—and he will make a positive one concerning your product or service.

16. Factory workers

Factory workers want security for themselves and their families. They are money-conscious and guarded. Price is important to them, so appeal to them on this level. They need to see proof of any claims about the product. The closer must not be too pushy because this customer is quite suspicious of salespeople. Focus on affordability, guarantees, and financing terms. No matter how he is dressed or sounds, maintain respect for this customer and never let him perceive you are talking down to him or you'll lose the sale. They are very used to having this happen and obviously don't like it. Treat him right and he'll buy.

17. Farmers

Farmers are often strong individualists. They can make a decision when they want to, but they are independent and open-minded. They are personable and understanding, and they will usually give people the benefit of the doubt. They can be closed by using logic, friendship, and a positive, enthusiastic sales presentation. They will buy hard if they believe in the close.

18. First responders (firefighters, paramedics, and so on)

Many firefighters are personable and understanding. They have open minds but are cautious and security-oriented. They are independent in their thinking and can make quick buying decisions. They generally want a good deal and are excellent on referrals. They are buyers all the way. They can best be closed by showing respect for their job. The closer should also present the product with enthusiasm, emphasizing the advantages of ownership. The closer should eagerly listen to any "war stories" that the customer can be persuaded to share.

19. Government workers

Government employees are not necessarily self-motivated and may require leadership. They can get excited and enthused if shown the advantages of the product or service. They are security-minded, but can be turned into impulse buyers. They can often be closed by using pressure in a low-key presentation. They can also be successfully intimidated into buying. The closer can use enthusiasm to a great extent, but should always be pushing toward a final, quick close—before they have a chance to change their minds.

20. Judges

They can be conservative and deliberate in their decision-making. They are, needless to say, careful buyers with optimistic attitudes. They work with logic and reason and cannot be pressured. They can be closed by showing a great deal of respect for their profession. They should be given a positive, enthusiastic, honest sales presentation. The closer should show professionalism and courtesy at all times. Judges have seen it all and are good at spotting phonies. Don't try to oversell this razor-sharp consumer.

21. Lawyers

Some lawyers tend to have "know-it-all" attitudes. They are aggressive and they will make a decision when necessary but often have to be motivated and led. They can be closed by working on their egos and carefully building them up. The closer can use positive pressure and should show professionalism so the buyer doesn't think he is simply another fast-talking "salesman." Be careful with your presentation, as a slick lawyer will often try to catch you in a white lie or exaggeration.

22. Managers/administrators

Believe it or not, managers and administrator types often have to be led into a decision. They are personable but feel out of place when not in their own environment. By and large, they are not especially open-minded but can be gently pressured into a sale. They are not overly optimistic, but can be motivated to buy sooner than they otherwise might by showing respect for their job and the high responsibility they hold. Massage their egos and show parallels between your job and theirs, but always acknowledge that their job probably contains greater complexities than yours. Use pressure and bring up the fact that decision-making must be a major part of their responsibility, so it must be easier for them to make buying decisions than for the average customer.

23. Mechanics

Mechanics are hard workers who also play hard. They want improvements to their quality of life and security for their families. They are open-minded when it comes to a good, and they will buy if convinced of the product's or service's quality. They are personable and trusting to some degree. Mechanics can be closed by giving an enthusiastic and exciting sales presentation. In most cases, they respond to emotion more than logic. They will buy all the way if they are motivated and believe in the advantages you have presented. They can be pressured in a positive, low-key manner.

24. Military personnel—officers

Military officers like to know they are in control and making the decision. They are open-minded when they think they are respected and that they're the center of attention. They can make a quick decision, and often will. They can be motivated easily when the ego is played upon because they are sold on themselves and their own leadership abilities. They can be closed by making them feel they have elicited more information from you than other people have. Let them feel they are on the inside concerning the sale, buying because of their own knowledge about the product.

25. Military personnel—enlisted

Enlisted military personnel are buyers all the way. They can become interested and excited about your product with little effort on your part. They are optimistic, have a lot of faith in their future, and are looking for a good deal and will show you a lot of trust. They can be effectively pressured, and do require a bit of leadership. Enlisted men can be closed if you give them an enthusiastic sales presentation. Show this customer respect and friendliness.

26. Clergy members

In my experience, some clergy members expect a super-discount or to be treated specially because of their obvious contribution to society. They can be pressured into buying, but have a tendency to cancel. They can be led and motivated easily. They think optimistically and are usually personable because of their vocation and experience with people. They can be closed with gentle pressure and a little intimidation. They can be trapped easily with a positive sales presentation. With this customer, the closer can be aggressive, as long as he is also respectful of the customer's beliefs. These customers expect they will not be lied to, and they are sophisticated when it comes to judging people. Be straight with these influential customers and they will come back to you many times over.

27. Nurses

Nurses are proud of their profession and will make a decision if they are even slightly motivated. They are aggressive and more likely to think about most products or services with optimism than with pessimism. They are open-minded and personable and react best to a friendly sales presentation. They can be closed by using a positive, upbeat approach. The closer has to use enthusiasm and show respect for this profession. The closer can use logic, but emotions work far better.

28. Physicians

Many doctors are thinkers and will buy eventually—if shown logic and the financial advantages of the product or service. The closer can sell almost any doctor if he shows he is a professional and handles himself in a respectable manner. The closer should work on ego, addressing the customer as "doctor" and not "doc." He also must show control and not be overly impressed by people's titles and credentials. Also, note that doctors have the well-deserved reputation of being terrible businessmen. It is true. They've been taken many times before, but you must be sure to be aboveboard in your dealings and in your presentation, or they will place you in the same category as the many dishonest salespeople they've had problems with in the past.

29. Law enforcement personnel

People in law enforcement think in a skeptical manner and often try to find fault with sales presentations and with products. They are proud of their profession and will show it. Policemen can be good customers if some kind of common bond or friendship is established.

They like to do business with people who demonstrate an appreciation for what they do. An enthusiastic, exciting sales presentation should be used. Friendliness works well with this type of customer, as he does not have the chance to be too friendly on the job.

30. Professors

These are usually very conservative customers. Professors are most definitely thinkers. They are "mull-it-over" customers. They are not excitable and are very low-key. They will often ask questions about the product or service that no one else would ever think about. They can be closed by showing respect, and by building up their egos. They should be complimented on their questions about your product or service, no matter how far-out they may be. The closer should try to learn something from these customers, or at least make the customers think they are. Professors should always be shown a positive, enthusiastic sales presentation.

31. Retired people

Retired individuals are often concerned about their futures. They are usually on a limited income and will be ultraconservative buyers. They are slow in their acquisition habits, and in their decision-making policies. They will not jump into anything. They will be fairly passive to most enthusiastic, aggressive sales presentations. Surprisingly, they can be closed by giving an exciting and enthusiastic sales presentation at first, just to get their full attention; then, by showing logic and the soft sell, the closer can develop emotions and spirit in this customer. The closer should attempt to inspire trust, using sincerity and understanding with his retired potential buyers. These customers are excellent for referrals because they often live in communities with many other retired people who will rely on recommendations of their friends.

32. Salespeople

Believe it or not, salespeople can be sold just about anything. They are generally aggressive and independent. They are positive thinkers and will make an impulse decision when buying. They are motivated and optimistic—always looking for a good deal and thinking that they will find one. They can best be closed by making them feel they know the inside story concerning the product. The closer needs to carefully build up their egos and show enthusiasm and respect for their sales knowledge and the fact that they are also in the business of selling. The closer should first gently build up the salespeople and then let them trap themselves. Intimidation and pressure will usually not work because they use the same bag of tricks and will know exactly what you are up to.

33. Schoolteachers

Teachers are used to talking and will show that in their conversation with you. They generally think in a conservative manner and will not jump into something until they really understand it. They are not overly optimistic in their thinking. They can be closed by showing respect for their profession, and it helps to get them talking about their favorite student stories. They can often be pressured into buying. The closer should work on ego while giving a positive, low-key, highly credible presentation.

34. Small business owners

Small business owners will often make quick decisions and stand by them. They are aggressive, self-motivated, optimistic thinkers. When it comes to referrals, they are so-so. This customer understands your problem. He is often running his own company and doing much of the selling as well. To close these customers, all you need is a very positive, logical sales presentation. The closer should show plenty of enthusiasm and excitement. Be professional, work on this customer's ego, and show respect for his accomplishments. Use a little showmanship, but keep in mind that this customer is usually razor-sharp and often sales-oriented himself.

There are many professions not mentioned here, but the ideas are basic. Customers are individuals and must be approached as such. The master closer has to deal with each of his customers on an individual level. He must alter the presentation according to his observations about their needs. The more he understands what their needs are, the better he will be able to close them. The best closers customize each pitch to the identifiable preferences of his clients. The secret is to properly analyze each customer before saying too much. There are no short cuts in successful selling, so don't expect to cut corners if you want to be the best.

I've never met a customer whose money had a mind of its own.

—Jim Pelphrie, Brisbane, Australia

Special note: Master one minute closers never forget one important thought that many customers carry around with them during the sales presentation: "If you, Mr. Closer, had listened hard enough the first time I spoke, then you, Mr. Closer, might have heard what I meant to say."

Part IV
How Master One Minute Closers Prepare for Their Customers

Customers are opportunities more so
than they are challenges.

—Rita Denton, Orlando, Florida

In this part of the book, we'll see how master closers get mentally prepared to meet their customer for the first time. We'll look at every step they take to greet their customers in the most positive and accommodating way.

Every master closer has his or her own unique habits, rituals, or private ceremonies to help ensure he or she gets a sale. Some of these practices have value and are recorded here. The following facts do not come from sales managers, or any sales meetings. They come from the master closers themselves; the folks on the front line who take no prisoners.

Before continuing, we should look at the exact definition of closing. Closing is a plan, a design, tactic, or maneuver with which the master closer puts his customer into a position in which the customer has to make a buying decision. In other words, the customer is put into a physiological corner, and he has to say either, "Yes, I'll buy," or "No, I won't."

Every little sales step leads toward a deal. Leave one step out
and you take one step back, away from the sale.

—*Lisa Rogers, New York, New York*

FACT 1. Logic versus emotions

When it comes to purchasing a product, human emotions will always play a much greater role than logic.
Most people around the world tend to buy with their
heart rather than their brain. The reason is simple. Master closers get the customer to emotionally feel and appreciate the product, with all its advantages, prestige,
possibilities, and self-serving applications, rather than
just explaining and exhibiting a lot of product details,
manufacturing information, and "slick" brochures. In
other words, the master puts the customer into the
driver's seat more times that he puts the customers'
head under the hood. Master closers work at getting
their customers involved with the product and excited
about purchasing. They want customers to jump around,
hug, shake hands, smile, and basically feel great, because they know that customers are going to show their
friends what they bought, and that showing off something they are proud of not only satisfies their ego, but
makes the deal solid and creates an avenue for new
referrals. In any sales presentation, when customers get
fully wrapped up in the whirlwind enthusiasm of the
closer, they will usually buy. Remember, if a person in

sales has any doubts about the product he's selling, or doesn't have a passion for that product, he needs to find another job immediately.

The master closer who works by himself is always ready to sell, but the closer who works with another always has to wait.

—Jon Roper, Pretoria, South Africa

FACT 2. Program office personnel

The master closer recognizes and addresses every person who works in or around his sales office by his or her first name. He goes out of his way to appreciate everyone and knows a little something about their families. The master has tactfully cultivated all who come in contact with him, leading them to speak kindly to him and always have a positive and pleasant greeting for him.

Now, the closer has purposely orchestrated this friendly atmosphere for a very important reason, and that is, when the closer is walking around the sales office, inside or out, with his customer, all the people who have gotten into the daily habit of saying "hello" and being kindhearted toward him will do just that, which, in turn, makes the closer look as if he's important and respected. This, of course, has a very reassuring effect on the customer, giving the customer a warmer feeling for the closer and subconsciously filling the customer with thoughts like, "I'm glad we got this salesperson, everyone likes him," or, "This salesperson seems like someone who can get things done." And with good thoughts like these running through the customer's mind, what more could a closer ask for? By programming everyone around the office, the master closer has made himself look good in front of the customer, without saying a word.

Special note: The master closer will also get everyone in the sales office in the habit of using the word "today." For instance, "How are you doing today?" "Isn't it gorgeous out today?" "You look good today," and so on. Reader, anything can be overdone, so moderation is the key, but you get the point. When the word "today" is used around the customer, the subliminal message will sink in, and the customer, at some point during the sales presentation, will start to realize the closer expects to get business done "today."

A good sales presentation is 20 percent preparation and 80 percent theater.

—*Judy Cain, Orlando, Florida*

FACT 3. Master closers sell so con men can't

This is an unwritten rule all master closers abide by: "The deal stops with them." Master closers know for a fact that if their customers don't buy from them, chances are they will go somewhere else to purchase, and the people they buy from could very well con, hurt, and swindle them out of their hard-earned money. The master has a responsibility to his customers. He should, with every power of persuasion he possesses, try to get his customers sold. This self-ordained obligation stems from the fact the master closer has studied his competition and knows his product is the best. He has seen other customers in the past make mistakes by buying from disreputable companies, then return to him with horror stories.

When a master closer truly believes his product is perfectly fit for his customer, he has every right to push, prod, and pressure for a sale. There are thousands of great salespeople in the world blessed with the talent of persuasion, but they have unfortunately turned their abilities into weapons to cheat and defraud people. Professional one minute closers know all the tricks of the trade, but they'll never purposely do a fraudulent transaction. Master closers protect their customers with truth. They have a fiduciary obligation and will do everything, within reason, to sell their good product so the con man down the road can't sell his.

All a con man really wants is the chance to prey on some unsuspecting customer, and he won't have that chance if the customer has already purchased where his money is safe, and he has peace of mind.

What the master closer does for himself in life will die with him, but what he does for his customers will live forever.

—Terry Nelson, London, United Kingdom

FACT 4. The past means nothing, today means everything

Before meeting any new customer, the master closer will mentally prepare himself by thinking, "Today means everything, and all of yesterday's tribulations, disappointments, and victories mean nothing." Now, the master will remember, and mentally note, past experiences that could benefit him in the future, but he will not dwell on them. Instead he will deliberately focus only on today, a valued "new beginning," offering the opportunity to sell his next customer. Below is a note written one hundred years ago in southern Italy. It was penned by a sea captain and has been translated from Italian into English.

Today, at this very place and time, will be the only guaranteed opportunity I will ever be blessed with to change the way I think and act. Right now, at this one given moment, I can rediscover and rekindle the true me, that somehow or some way got lost, tarnished, maybe even broken in a world indifferent to individual hurts. All of my yesterdays have gifted or burdened me with success, failure, joy, and grief. None everlasting, and none really forgotten. As for tomorrow, it gives hope, the foundation for dreams, and tomorrow hints of promise, but never offering that inner calm or comfort needed for peaceful rest, that rest I've always wanted, always sought. I realize today is all that matters, because today is reality, and its directness is visible in all that surrounds. Its hours and minutes are lived and its possibilities unlimited. Today is given to me as a merciful chance. One more gracious grant to be all. If I let forever or later steal my set resolve, then I have foolishly gambled away God's gift.

Take pride in your work, prove yourself on every play, have dedication, and have a good time, and the score will take care of itself.

—*Frank Broyles, University of Arkansas, Fayetteville, Arkansas*

<u>FACT 5.</u> Never think about money

The very last thing a master closer wants to think about before he meets his customer is money. He knows if he has a commission, spiff, or bonus on his mind, it will show, and the customer can tell. The quotation from Frank Broyles is true in sports and in business. If a master closer just relaxes, enjoys his work and his customer, while believing in his product, everything else will fall into place. Nothing can beat enthusiasm, friendship, and honesty. The only reason a customer won't buy when facing such opponents is the money, and this is a condition no one but the customer can solve.

In life, as on a tightrope, stand as tall and straight as you can, just don't lose your balance.

—*Judy Tatman, Detroit, Michigan*

FACT 6. Customers need the closer's energy

When customers first meet a closer, they are full of energy, but it's the wrong kind of "energy." Their movements and liveliness come from anxiety and apprehension, two harmful elements the closer must tactfully address and destroy.

Note: How to disarm and make the customer feel comfortable will be discussed in Part V of this book.

Now, unless the master closer can win over the customer in the first several minutes of their initial meeting, the customer will most likely go through the whole sales presentation without really hearing or understanding a thing. Another thought that plays on the customer's mind, making him feel uneasy and giving him even more negative energy, is the realization that he could meet a closer who does not have his interest at heart. The master will use his personality and make friends with the customer from the very start. Then he will methodically build up trust and slowly turn any negative energy into positive energy and excitement. The customer needs the closer's "can do" attitude all the way through the sales presentation, so that when it comes time to make a buying decision, the customer has enough self-confidence and strength to fearlessly purchase the product. If the master closer fails to transmit his excitement and positive energy to his customer, there will be no sale. It's as simple as that.

There is an old Chinese tale that pretty much explains what we are talking about.

A long time ago, there was this rusty old shield that had been leaning against a giant forest tree for over one hundred years. Now, over these past one hundred years, the shield had made friends with the sun. Every morning and evening, the sun and the shield would greet each other, and during the day, would have pleasant conversations. Well, one day the sun looked down on his old friend the shield and noticed that the shield was very sad, and didn't want to talk. The sun kept bothering and pestering the shield, asking what was wrong, until the shield finally answered and told his friend, the sun, his trouble. The shield explained that he once was a beautiful and respected shield, that all armies feared and admired, but over the past one hundred years, after being left in the forest all alone, he had become rusty, dull, and unappreciated. This was the reason he was so sad and depressed. His friend, the sun, just smiled and told him not to worry. The sun looked directly at the shield and said, "You are my friend, you don't have to feel bad. You are still that great shield, and to prove it, all you have to do, my friend, is just polish yourself up and reflect me."

Reader, it's the same way with closers and customers. All the customer has to do, once he feels at ease, is reflect the powers of the closer, and just like magic, you have two parties in harmony, showing the same level of enthusiasm and emotion. Now, when this happens, and it will, there will be a sale made.

The difference between a closer and a conversationalist is that the conversationalist will make friends, while the closer will make friends and get deals. Any salesman can talk, but only closers can talk, calculate, plan, inspire, rearrange, realign, discover, plot, emphasize, sympathize, adjust, and sell.

—*Tyne Kosimo'se, Tokyo, Japan*

FACT 7. Three major reasons customers buy

There are only three major reasons customers buy. The first is desire. If the customer wants the product, knows the product will be useful, understands the product is a sound investment, believes and likes the closer, then he'll buy. The second reason people buy is money. The customer needs to know the product being sold is priced fairly, and the customer needs to know the price will fit into his budget. The third major reason the customer will buy is that he has given himself permission to purchase. He has reasoned to himself that he needs the product, or he knows that when he buys the product people close to him will approve.

*Note: Inside every customer there is a subtle fear others might make
fun of him for buying a certain product, or people he respects
might get upset. The customer wants his family and friends to
endorse the purchase. This is just another way of saying that he
has permission from all who might be concerned.*

If a customer feels comfortable in all three of these
areas, desire, money, and permission, he will buy the
product and be a satisfied customer.

If you've never lost, then you've never won.

—Jim Williams, Dallas, Texas

FACT 8. Listen to the customer

Every closer knows to listen to his or her customer.
That's elementary. But master closers know to listen
more deeply. For instance, when a customer tells the
closer he is a good or bad person, chances are the
customer is telling the truth. If a customer discloses to
the closer a secret or describes himself the way he sees
himself, the closer had better pay attention because
the customer is saying what he truly believes. Most
customers, at some point during the sales presentation, provided they trust the closer, will confide in the
master. If the master closer is alert to every little hint,
sooner or later, the customer will reveal his true character, and when that happens, the master will know
exactly how to sell (close) him.

People need at least a three foot protective space surrounding them to feel comfortable among strangers.

—*Dr. Lenn Hickmen, New York, New York*

FACT 9. Never tell customers what they should do

Never tell customers what they should do, rather inspire them and encourage them to do what they already know they should do. Customers generally know what they want and are looking for in a product. All the master closer has to do is discover what customers' needs are and then subtly point them in the right direction, while at the same time influencing them to follow through with their desire and buy. When master closers take this approach to any customer, the results are astonishing. Customers treated in this manner think they are in control and running the show. This allows the customer to act braver than he normally would. Don't forget, the master closer never loses control, he only makes the customer think he's piloting the plane.

Note: In Part VII of this book, controlling customers will be explained in detail.

When a customer wants a certain product, and the master closer just gives that extra gentle push, while reinforcing all the positives the customer is thinking, then if money is not the problem, a sale will be made.

There is no such thing as security, but there is opportunity, and it requires work.

—*Win Lochee, Hong Kong, China*

FACT 10. Money will always be the issue

If every master closer in the world gave his product away, and customers wouldn't have to pay one cent, the closer's whole line of product, no matter what it was, would be gone in less than an hour. Master closers know, after everything is said and done, provided the master did his job, the only reason people won't buy his product is that they can't afford it. It doesn't matter how many excuses or stories the customer comes up with, in almost every case, money will be the bottom-line problem. If a customer doesn't have the money to purchase the product, this is a condition the closer cannot overcome. Master closers can defeat any objection a customer throws at him, except the issue of "no funds." When a master faces this condition, he will not embarrass the customer, but will be understanding and let the customer go with dignity. All the closer can salvage from this experience is the knowledge that the customer would have bought if the product had been affordable.

Love everyone, but don't trust anyone.

—*Unknown*

FACT 11. (Important) How a customer treats others

How someone treats other people is just a reflection of how he feels about himself. This is a statement all master closers understand. This one fact alone helps masters recognize, interpret, and understand each customer they greet, before the customer even says one word. For example, if a customer walks into a sales office with a chip on his shoulder, and is mean or rude to everyone he meets, he's got a problem that he alone has to live with every minute of his life. The truth is this: If a customer treats others in an unpleasant way, he treats himself the same way and just doesn't like himself. On the other side of the coin, if a customer enters a sales environment and is truly jovial and friendly toward everyone, this customer loves himself. No matter how the customer acts, the master closer can tell a great deal about him from his interactions with others. Remember the golden rule of relationships, "Be sad with sad people, and happy with happy people," because when an emotional connection is made, true progress in communication and fellowship can flourish.

Most master closers always expect the best, but sometimes they're disappointed. Then there are salespeople who only expect the worst, and they are always disappointed.

—*Ty Kellyman, Melbourne, Australia*

Note: "Clearing the mind." Before meeting any new customer, master closers clear their minds of everything except selling.

They will not think of what happened last night, yesterday, or the day before. They will not worry about any personal problem or sales office situation. The only thing they will concentrate on is their customer. This might sound strange to someone not in the business, but when a closer gets a deal, all other matters seem inconsequential. There is nothing like getting a sale, because the feeling it creates overpowers and tends to erase any and all problems.

If a master closer meets his customer acting half-hearted and depressed, it can be guaranteed he will not come close to getting a deal, unless it's a planned closing maneuver. To help illustrate this thought there is an old Japanese story about seven Buddhist monks who were making a pilgrimage to a temple high in the mountains. They had been on this journey for several weeks when they came to a wide river. On the bank of the river, they saw, sitting alone on a large rock, a beautiful maiden. They asked if they could help her in any way, and she told them she wanted to cross the river but was afraid. The monks agreed to assist, and four of them carried her across safely. After they made sure she would be all right, they left and continued on their way. Later that night, when the monks made camp, some of them, for the first time, started arguing and yelling, and getting upset with each other. That's when one of the older monks approached the elder of the group and asked the leader, "Why are our brothers having these problems all of a sudden? Why is every-one not getting along?" The elder monk looked at his old friend and said, "Our brothers did not leave the maiden at the river."

If I expect to get a good customer, I will. If I think I'll get a bad customer, I do, but if I believe I'll sell, I can.

—*Chris Sampier, Nassau, Bahamas*

Part V

Act 1:
How Master One Minute Closers Introduce Themselves and Their Product to Customers

The professional master closer builds his reputation
by helping other closers build theirs.

—Jerry Fisher, Boston, Massachusetts

Now, we'll look at how the master one minute closer thinks and acts when he meets a customer and introduces his product to that customer for the first time. Many sales books have been written on how "first impressions are lasting impressions." Well, that's not necessarily so. Just because a closer and a customer don't click right away, the relationship isn't necessarily doomed. With a little effort on the closer's part—striking up some warm-up conversation, asking questions in order to know one another better—the closer can win the customer over. "Off on the wrong foot" relationships can be transformed. Reader, before making any judgment about others, get to know and try to understand them. Nine times out of ten, you won't regret it.

In school, we learn lessons to take tests, but in real life, we're tested to learn lessons.

—*Don Downum, London, United Kingdom*

<u>FACT 1.</u> Master closers are punctual and they take control

When the master closer first meets his customer, he will always be on time or early for the meeting. The reason, besides being respectful to the customer, is that anyone who is late has to first (before saying anything), apologize for the tardiness, which psychogically gives the person who was on time and waiting the upper hand. For anyone to start a meeting with the words "I'm sorry" or "forgive me for not being on time" automatically puts that person at a disadvantage.

There is a very powerful and secret technique master closers can employ in meetings. This trick not only enables the master closer to take immediate control of the meeting, but also allows the master to learn a lot of valuable information about the customer—private information that the customer probably never dreamed he would be telling a stranger. It is called the "tell-all technique," and here's how it works. When a master has a meeting with a customer or any person, he makes sure he's a few minutes early. Then, when the customer arrives (early, on time, or late, it doesn't matter), the master closer will look directly at the customer with a slight look of concern on his face and ask, before offering any type of greeting or shaking hands, "What happened?" The first natural response the customer will give is, "What do you mean, what happened?" (Reader, this is where the magic comes in.) Then, again, with the same concerned look on his face, the master will ask the customer, "What happened?" The second time the customer hears the same question, the customer will, for one or two seconds, think to himself, "What does this guy mean? I wonder if he somehow knows what I did last night or he found out what I did this morning. Maybe I had better not lie to him, because he already apparently knows something." It's at this split-second that he decides not to take any chances on what the master might or might not know and tells the closer everything that has happened to him in the past twelve hours. For example, the customer will say something like, "Well, when I got up this morning, I couldn't find my car keys, but truthfully I thought my son might have taken the car last night without my permission. So, I was in a rush and kind of upset, and the whole day has been hectic." From the customer's spontaneous and off-guard response the master closer takes mental notes, remembering every little fact the customer reveals about himself. Then, after the customer's explanation is over, the master will immediately be cordial, shake hands, and direct the customer to his office, or whatever location he wants. In this "tell-all" trick, the master closer has learned a lot of "extras" about the customer, has made the customer feel the master knows and sees all, and the master closer, before even saying "Good morning" or "Hello; how are you?" has taken complete control of the customer, which instantly disarms him. In my experience, this "What happened?" techinique works about

90 percent of the time. All the master closer has to do is act serious and play the part.

It's kind of funny, but in learning sales techniques, it usually takes a long time to find a shorter way.

—Honi Monchiea, Tokyo, Japan

FACT 2. Number one rule, never prejudge others concerning money

Every sales book on the market preaches, "Never prejudge anyone," and that is the truth. But master closers know one very important fact that few if any sales books disclose. That is that people with money, meaning real money, old money, don't flaunt it, because they don't want others to know how rich they are. The folks who deliberately show their money off, in cars and jewelry, often don't have as much as they would have others believe. In fact, they are, in a lot of cases, living on the edge of financial disaster. People with money can be very reserved and, most of the time, very pleasant and cordial. The master closer should understand that, because he usually won't discover a customer's true financial position until much later in the sales presentation.

Note: Don't forget, any time during the sales presentation, the customer, if asked, could decide to purchase, and the master closer is always prepared with pen and worksheet or contract to immediately stop everything he is doing, not say another word, and write up the agreement. Also, to break the ice when signing a contract, the master closer always signs his name first, and then hands the pen to the customer so he can sign, saying, "Mr. Customer, I need your name right next to mine." This simple but important exercise works wonders for the customer's comfort level. On the other hand, if the customer indicates he would like to buy the closer's product, and the closer spontaneously produces a contract and says, "Just sign here," handing the customer a pen, the customer, in most instances, will immediately get nervous, have second thoughts, and decide to wait or not buy at all.

Never break a customer's "bubble." If a customer wants to be president, then say, "How are you, Mr. President?"

—*Gary Thompson, Vancouver, Canada*

FACT 3. Go unarmed

Master closers never approach a new customer with a pen in hand, with one showing in the pocket, or with an armload of product information and papers. The customer has enough anxieties and "unknowns" going through his mind as it is, and he sure doesn't need to be unnerved further by seeing a closer coming his way weighed down with documents and brochures, which can be perceived as weapons of mass destruction. If this sounds silly, or like nonsense, just imagine people sitting in the waiting room of a dentist's office, and all of a sudden, a door opens, and the dentist is standing there with a big hypodermic needle in hand and asks,

"Who's next?" Well, I can tell you one thing, it won't be this author.

The master's first obligation to his customer is to make him calm, let the customer realize he is not going to be threatened, and get the customer involved in friendly nonintrusive conversation. Master closers can disarm any guarded customer with soft and interesting dialogue, nothing more, and nothing less.

Winning . . . will not be entrusted to the weak or the timid.

—*Mack Brown, coach of University of Texas football*

<u>FACT 4.</u> The right eye only

Important: This is a secret acting trick all master closers use. When actors are filmed they are trained to look only at the right eye of the actor facing them. The reason is that, when the camera is rolling, if an actor, when delivering his lines, keeps moving his eyes, looking at the other actors' eyes, this eye movement will disrupt the integrity of the scene. Again, actors are instructed to look at the right eye of another actor to keep the eye steady, so there won't be extra visual interference that might take away from the dialogue being delivered. Master closers have embraced this acting method when talking to customers. When a master looks only into the right eye of his customer, the customer can't tell which eye the closer is focusing on, and the customer will feel the intensity and power of each word the master closer says. This "right eye" contact is so subtle, and so full of concentrated energy, that the customer's subconscious picks it up, which, in turn, makes the customer, without even knowing it, listen to what the master closer is saying with a lot more interest.

Always listen to what a woman says with her eyes.

—Dlies Chowlee, Hong Kong, China

Special note: When a customer is seated at the master closer's desk and won't make eye contact with the master, the one minute closer will lightly tap his pen on the desk getting the attention of the customer. When the customer looks at the tapping pen, the closer will slowly raise the pen to his eye level, bringing the customer's eyes in contact with the closer's. It's at this point eye contact is made and the closer can continue with his presentation with all participants involved.

FACT 5. The double acknowledgment handshake

Sales people know to give the customer a firm handshake, but the master closer has perfected the "greeting handshake" to an art that makes the customer feel even more welcome and appreciated than a normal handshake does. Here is how the master closer shakes hands with his customer. One second after the master grasps the customer's hand, he looks down at the handshake, silently acknowledging it, and one second later looks back into the customer's right eye. Then, two or three seconds later, the master releases his hand from the firm but friendly grip and carries on as normal. What this one glance at the handshake does is remarkable. The customer will absolutely notice it and the closer's extra effort. The customer will not be startled by the closer's handshake "look," but will be impressed by the subtle but deliberate gesture. As the customer sees it, it's a courteous glance to reconfirm that the handshake is a good and solid one. The special handshake gesture is as powerful as a kind hand placed on the shoulder by an old friend from school or an old army buddy. This exercise is simple and takes only seconds, but the results are astonishing. The customer will instantly relate to the closer and will warm up to him much faster than he would if the closer had just shaken his hand and started talking.

Note: The double acknowledgment handshake can also be used after the customer agrees to purchase. It's a very strong technique that helps solidify the deal.

FACT 6. Touching customers

If a master closer has the habit of touching his customer on the arm or forearm while he is talking, he must inform the customer about his friendly habit the very first time they meet. If the closer is a "toucher" and fails to address this point, the customer could become irritated during the sales presentation and never pay attention to anything the closer is saying, much less buy the closer's product. Customers are very sensitive to every move the closer makes, and they sure don't like upsetting surprises. The master closer must remember his customer has most likely been to other sales companies and has not purchased, for some unknown reason. So, the customer is educated and wise to "silver-tongued" salespeople and their "slap-on-the-back" methods. That is why it's important that the master be sincere and honest when dealing with his customers, because he wants to be pleasantly different from previous salespeople his customers have said "no" to.

All customers expect to be treated like a friend, but few expect to find a friend.

—*Marc Leotainie, Rome, Italy*

FACT 7. Address everyone in the customers' party

When a customer arrives at a sales office, or is approached by a salesman at his home, if he has a large family or another couple with him, many times the salesperson will mistakenly focus only on the individual he thinks has the money, or the folks he thinks will make the final buying decision.

Note: Now, if a closer wants to split up two couples, feeling that one of the couples could jeopardize the sale, that's the closers call. He has that right.

When the master closer is faced with a large group, and he chooses to mass pitch, he will under no circumstances ignore anyone. He will give his total sales presentation enthusiastically addressing everyone, even children. The master knows that, for a customer to feel comfortable and purchase, he needs and wants the consent of people close to him.

Again, many times, salespeople will give all of their attention to the one person they believe holds the purse strings, and in many cases, they will be correct, except for one oversight. It is possible that another person in the customer's party doesn't have the money, but does have the final say. So, for this reason, master closers give their all to all, never underestimating anything or anyone. It's always better to play it safe at first, and pitch everyone, than to try to get it all sorted and figured out too early during the sales presentation, when relationships could get strained, complicated, or just blow up.

Teach your customers to love themselves.

—*Hans Stickel, Wiesbaden, Germany*

Note: Many master closers will program their customers about their sales presentation. They will tell the customers how they will first explain the product, then show the product, and finally describe how other people have purchased the product. Closers will forewarn the customer, in a gentle and business-as-usual manner, that they will show prices and buying advantages at the end of the presentation, so there are no hidden surprises.

FACT 8. Control the customer's emotions

The master closer will, during the whole sales presentation, control his customer's emotions. If the closer loses control of a customer, letting the customer's feelings and whims rule the day, all is lost. The closer must direct and influence nearly everything the customers thinks and does during the presentation, or things could become confused, disorganized and unpredictable.

For instance, if a customer first meets the closer in a sales office with too much enthusiasm, then in most cases, the closer has a "stroker," "tire kicker," or "phony" on his hands. The closer must settle this type of customer down and make him understand that he, the closer, is serious about his business and generally get the customer thinking in realistic terms.

Note: We are only talking about new customers here, not referrals. Referrals usually have their own special attitude and think differently than new customers.

Another example concerning customers' emotions: Let's say a closer meets a customer and the customer doesn't want to say a word, or the customer acts very negative toward everything the closer does or says. In a case like this, the master will get on the same emotional level as the problem customer, bond, show empathy, and convince the customer he understands the emotions exhibited. Then, using his powers of persuasion and positive personality, he will bring the customer up to a comfortable level where real and tangible business can be conducted in a sober and timely fashion. The master closer will always find a way to control the customer's emotions.

You either control the customer, or the customer controls you.

—*Bill Willbanks, Chicago, Illinois*

FACT 9. Double bonding

Salespeople are taught and know that common interests create bonds, but master closers know common interests create bonds, but a passion for that interest embraces. There is a big difference. All salespeople, when they first meet their customer, try to find some kind of common ground or interest, so they can develop and carry on a "warm-up" conversation. Master closers do the same thing, but in greater detail, and encourage kinsmanship, which creates a better and more lasting harmony for the "closer/customer" relationship. For example, when a master closer meets his customer, and they start talking, the master will ask the customer where he is from, and the customer will answer, "I'm from Dallas, Texas." The master will say: "That's where my family is from, Dallas." At this point, there has been a common interest found, but the master takes it one giant step further. The master closer will continue and ask, "What part of Dallas do

you live in?" The customer answers, "We live in Highland Park," and the master says, telling the truth, "That's
where my family lives, in Highland Park." The customer
will immediately feel as if he has met an old friend,
because the closer knows his neighborhood personally,
and that usually translates into a sale, as the customer
feels more relaxed and at ease with a closer who can
talk his language. Remember, the master closer will go
beyond the general "common interest" format and find
a deeper related interest that brings the customer and
master even closer together.

*Note: Always tell the truth. One little lie about anything will and
should kill a deal.*

Customers will forget most of what a closer said, but they'll
never forget how the closer made them feel.
                    —*Richard L. Davisen, Manchester, United Kingdom*

FACT 10. Repeat the last two words of what the customer says

This is a German master closer's trick, and it is powerful. This planned sales technique will get any customer
talking about himself, his family, his job, his finances,
or any other thing under the sun as long as the master
closer wants. This sales and one minute closing method
is used by the master to gather and mentally store any

and all information the customer voluntarily discloses. The most remarkable thing about this sales technique is that the customer doesn't even suspect the master is controlling the whole conversation and secretly pulling all the strings.

Here is how this sales method works: After the closer and customer meet and begin a light conversation, the closer will ask the customer a simple question. For example, "What do you do for a living?" The customer will answer, "I'm a truck driver for C. L. Smith." Then the closer will repeat back to the customer the last two words of the customer's last sentence. The master will say, making it a question, "C. L. Smith?" Now, when the customer hears the question, he'll think for a split-second, "This person doesn't know what I'm talking about, I had better explain more." The customer will automatically elaborate. "Yes, C. L. Smith, they're one of the largest trucking companies in the country." Then the closer again repeats back the last two words of the customer's last statement. The master closer will say, "The country?" The customer will again think to himself that the closer doesn't fully understand, so he, the customer, must explain, but this time in greater detail. The customer will elaborate further. "Yes, the country. C. L. Smith trucks are all over the United States, even in Canada and Mexico." Again, the closer will repeat back to the customer the last two words of his last statement, "In Mexico?" And again the customer will go into more detail. "Yes, Mexico. C. L. Smith Trucking travels everywhere. They are a very large and most respected company." Again, the closer says, "Respected company?" And the customer will again keep on talking, explaining and answering with more information every time the closer uses, as a question, the last two words of the customer's last sentence.

This question-and-answer process can go on for hours, and the customer will talk his head off, never knowing the closer was behind this information-gathering probe. Just remember, repeat back to the customer the last two words of his last sentence and watch the customer go on and on. The only time he'll stop talking is when the master decides not to ask any more "last two words of the sentence" questions.

Customers only understand what they have been prepared to understand.

—*Hans Krugger, Rotterdam, Netherlands*

FACT 11. Explaining the company and product

When a master closer is explaining his company's history, financial status, performance, future, and how long he has been with it, he will not put the customer to sleep with a lot of dry facts and figures. The master will break up this information with small and interesting stories, and if possible, spread the facts and reports throughout the whole sales presentation. Nothing will bore a customer more than having to sit through an orientation on the company's history.

The customer needs to understand the company and its products' history so he will feel comfortable spending his money. But, as the old saying goes, "If you confuse 'em, you lose 'em." And too many details will do just that. As every salesperson knows, keep it simple, entertaining, and to the point.

Note: When the customer asks a question concerning the company or really about anything, the master closer, even though he knows what the question will be, and knows the answer, will never "short stop" (that is, cut off a customer in midquestion) and give an answer. The master will patiently listen to the customer's whole question and then answer. Many times the customer will ask something that is completely opposite from what the closer thought was going to be asked, and by answering before the whole question was stated, the closer could come close to losing the sale. Remember, hear the customer completely out before saying or answering anything.

I sell because I answer three questions for my customers: "Why here?" "Why now?" and "Why you?"

—*Sam Rubrecht, Hilton Head, South Carolina*

I study sales so I can better understand what I know.

—*Sir Jerry Bensonhall, London, United Kingdom*

Part VI
Act 2:
How Master One Minute Closers Present Their Product to Customers

Customers will react positively to any product that makes them look and feel important.

—*Rog Malatra, Bombay, India*

Here we'll see how master one minute closers present their product to the customer. The master has already, in Act 1, oriented the customer about the product and what to expect. Now, he actually shows the product, so that the customer is not only hearing about the product, but seeing and touching it as well, which can help the customer develop an attachment to the product.

As I mentioned earlier, the customer, at any time, could decide to purchase, so the master closer must be prepared, with pen and worksheet or contract, to stop everything and immediately write up the sale.

Keep in mind that no product, no matter how great or well known it is, can sell itself. A product needs a spokesman, a representative, to herald its advantages, uses, and possibilities.

Stories and illustrations give meaning and purpose without ever having to explain meaning or purpose.

—*Su Sunming, Hong Kong, China*

FACT 1. Ask your enemy for a favor

There are times when a master closer will have a customer who just doesn't like anything or anyone. Throughout Act 1 of the sales presentation this kind of troublesome customer never paid attention, wasn't pleasant, and for some unknown reason, didn't like the master closer. If and when this unfortunate situation crops up, the master has an ingenious trick up his sleeve. This trick will make any enemy a friend in only a few minutes.

Note: Often a salesperson, when asked how to make friends with someone who doesn't like him, will answer, "Give him love and attention." Well, that might be a good answer in a 101 sales psychology class, but the trick the master closer uses is advanced, absolutely deadly, and not to be used by timid salespeople.

When the master closer is faced with a difficult customer, the master will put on a serious face and ask the customer in a most sincere and humble manner, "Please, Mr. Customer, would you do me a great favor?" The customer, out of natural human curiosity, will automatically say, "What?" or, "What do you want?" The master closer will ask the unfriendly customer to do something trivial, or something easy to do, anything the closer feels the customer would do if asked by anyone else, like close the window or the door, let him use the phone, loan him a pen, get a glass of water. When the customer obliges, something wonderful happens. The unkind customer, if only subconsciously, will instantly feel powerful and useful, feeling himself, in his own mind, more important than the closer who needed a favor of him. When the customer feels this way, he will go out of his way to be kinder and more considerate to the lowly closer. In a matter of minutes, the enemy, the customer, is now friendly to the needy and helpless closer. This kindness was created and deliberately set up by the master all along. This "ask-your-enemy-for-a-favor" trick works, but the master closer had better be a good actor, or things could easily fall apart and the situation could become uncomfortable.

If a customer says he understands too soon then the customer understands nothing.

—*Edmond Chambers, Pretoria, South Africa*

FACT 2. Let customers believe they are in control

By now, you know that the master closer is always in control, directing every move the customer makes, but all the while the customer believes he's in the driver's seat, which, of course, is only sound salesmanship. The master accomplishes this in several ways. For example, the master might say, "Mr. Customer, which product do you think would work for you?" or, "Mr. Customer, you know your finances better than anyone, just point me in the right direction." And sometimes, "Mr. Customer, it looks like you've done your homework, so I'll just hand the controls over to you and let you be the boss." Any statements similar to these will work wonders on a customer's ego. The customer will, to some degree, take control and usually show the closer exactly how to sell him, or he'll take control and get lost and confused. Either way, the master can pick up where he left off and tactfully direct the customer back toward a closing situation. Master closers will always make the customer feel paramount by listening to and respecting his questions, opinions, and statements.

No one respects a salesperson who talks badly about the competition, and no one will buy from someone he doesn't respect.

— *Sherry Watson, Palm Springs, California*

FACT 3. Respect the customer's questions

Customers ask questions because they want answers. Even though the master one minute closer has heard the same question a thousand times, he will patiently listen, hear the whole question, then answer. He will not, as stated earlier, cut the customer off. If he doesn't know the answer, he will tell the customer he doesn't know, congratulate the customer on asking such an intelligent question, then go and find the answer. Lazily making up an answer to pacify a customer is one of the the biggest mistakes one will ever make in sales. Sooner or later, that one lie, misrepresentation, or off-the-cuff remark will come back and bite. What's more, master closers look a lot more credible to their customers if they admit they don't have all the answers.

Customers' questions help keep the closer on his toes. No customer will buy something he doesn't understand, and if a salesperson can't satisfy the customer's inquires, the customer should purchase from someone who can. Customers have every right to learn everything they can about a product they might put their money into.

The only thing in sales that is more important than knowledge is imagination.

—*Diago Martin, Marbella, Spain*

FACT 4. Find out where you stand

Every salesperson knows this sales exercise, and all sales books mention it in one way or another. The reason this "find-out-where-you-stand" practice is looked at here is that master closers practice it, plus it's just a smart part of selling. The master will, throughout his sales presentation, take his customer's "temperature," to see how close or how far away he is from getting a sale. The master closer will ask the customer little questions to see what the response is. If a closer asks the customer if he likes the product so far, and the answer is, "Yes,

I like the product," the closer will, at that moment, ask the customer to buy. Now, if the customer says, "I'm not sure," the closer knows he still has work to do. The most important thing to remember is that, when the customer is excited about the product, and the master thinks the timing is right, the master closer will stop showing the product, and there on the spot ask the customer to buy. More times than one would expect, the customer will sign the worksheet or contract when asked.

The best and surest way to advise a customer is to find out what the customer really wants, then simply advise him to do it.

—*Scott McClain, Glasgow, Scotland*

FACT 5. Music versus Lyrics

Master closers realize most customers don't and can't comprehend all of the sales information they hear in the introduction part (Act 1) of the sales presentation. That's why, during the show and demonstration part (Act 2) of the presentation, the closer repeats what he previously said (in Act 1) concerning the product. This way, the customer not only sees, and if possible, touches the product, but also hears about its advantages and possibilities for a second time. This "second helping" lets the customer understand and assimilate the product that much better. It's a lot like what happens when people first hear a new song: They hear mostly the beat and tune, saying to themselves, "This is a nice song." Then, after hearing the song played two or three more times, they start paying more attention to the lyrics, not just the tune, and then say to themselves, "This really is a good song." Well, it's the same way with a sales presentation. The customer has to hear the description and dynamics of the product more than one time for it to really sink in. When the customer hears what the closer said in Act 1, then again in Act 2, while actually seeing and experiencing the product, the closer's words sound a lot different, and make more sense.

In step one, I show, in step two, I show and assist, in step three, I only encourage and let the other person reason on his own.

—*Master chef Ryan Dennis Johnson, Sedona, Arizona*

<u>FACT 6.</u> The customer must touch the product

It doesn't make any difference if the product being sold is something tangible or intangible. Even if it's only papers, brochures, or pamphlets, the customer must hold something so he can feel and experience the product. The reason is that when the customer actually touches the product, or something that represents the product, there is a silent bond made between customer and product. This is a very important step in getting a sale. The customer must get physically involved with the product in some way. If the customer only hears about the product without some kind of physical contact, the chances for a sale are greatly diminished.

Throughout Act 1, Act 2, and Act 3, the "closing phase," the closer is directing every emotion the customer has toward ownership.

Give customers what they want, even before they know they want it.

—*Philip Sanchez, Cancún, Mexico*

FACT 7. Do something pro bono for the customer

During the demonstration part of the sales presentation (Act 2), the master closer will find or make the time to do something kind and unexpected for his customer. He will go out of his way to assist or lend a hand to the customer, a kind gesture that will not go unnoticed.

For instance, the closer might watch the customer's children while he is out of the room, or help the customer get something out of his car. The closer does this friendly act, which should have nothing to do with the product, to be "neighborly" to the customer. Customers will respond in kind to any closer who will go beyond the call of duty, recognizing the closer gets nothing out of it except demonstrating his good nature.

Now, if a salesperson keeps strictly to business and performs like a robot, following a script or set list of rules and procedures, then the warmth that should exist between a customer and closer will be lost, most likely killing a sale.

Master closers have to show the customer their human side so the customer feels comfortable enough to show his. When both parties believe they know and understand each other, then the real business at hand will fall into place a lot sooner and smoother.

When a master closer has a man who won't listen, or acts uninterested, the best and fastest way to get him turned around and involved is for the master to start whispering to his wife.

—*J. M. McCurley, New Orleans, Louisiana*

FACT 8. Give pen to customer

This is another elementary sales lesson every salesperson knows, but it's so important that it bears repeating. At some convenient time during the sales demonstration (Act 2), the master closer will find a reason or way to hand his pen to the customer. There can be many valid excuses for this change of hands. For example, the closer could ask the customer to help him record some information regarding the product, or the closer could hand his pen to the customer for inspection, telling him it was a special gift (the closer has to be telling the truth), or the closer could tell the customer to take down his cell or home phone number for future reference, which is a maneuver to get the customer relaxed and lower his defenses, because now, with pen in hand, the customer thinks the closer has given up and he, the customer, is off the hook. Again, any legitimate reason the closer can think of for the pen exchange will be fine. Just remember, the importance of this exercise is to get the customer familiar and comfortable with the closer's pen, the very pen that will later be used in Act 3, the closing phase, to sign the contract.

Note: If the closer waits until the last minute and shows the pen to the customer at the wrong time or place, the sight of the pen could actually scare the customer and very possibly give him second thoughts about purchasing. The actual act of handing the pen over to the customer has to be very nonchalant and routine, nothing dramatic. The sooner the customer is familiar with this "deadly weapon" the better for all concerned.

Curiosity will take care of and overcome any boredom and apathy. Curiosity is one of the master closer's best friends.

—*Beth Simington, Brisbane, Australia*

FACT 9. Pictures through imagination

The master closer will not only put his customer into the driver's seat when demonstrating the product, but he will also paint pictures colored with imagination throughout the show-and-tell phase (Act 2). The master will explain to his customer all of the possibilities and privileges of ownership, and how advantageous it would be for his whole family. The master closer will tell personal stories, such as how ownership of the product has improved his own life, and he'll use every suitable avenue he can to direct and pull on the customer's emotions. The master closer is always pitching while subtly making the customer "thirsty" for his product.

If the customer doesn't ask questions, the closer hasn't done his job and the customer doesn't want the product.

—*Mary Sheldon, Dorchester, United Kingdom*

FACT 10. The transfer from show to close

For many salespeople, the transition from showing the product to getting the customer back into the sales office to close the deal is an awkward and delicate time. The real problem is the customer knows what's coming and will start to retreat into his defensive shell. The customer goes from talking openly to putting up his guard.

At this point, the master closer calmly tells the customer he wants to show him the financial benefits of owning the product, plus some important product information he has back in his office. Then the master simply directs the customer to his office without making a big fuss about it, acting as if it's business as usual.

Note: The simplest statement a master can make at this time is, "Mr. Customer, let me show you what this looks like on paper."

Now, if the closer has done his job correctly throughout the sales presentation (Act 1 and Act 2), taking the customer's temperature and keeping up the excitement and curiosity with a steady and deliberate momentum, this step will not be so nerve-wracking. Remember, the master explained to his customer earlier that after he had shown the product, he was going to write down exactly what the product cost and give the customer some additional information regarding the benefits of owning the product. By preprogramming the customer, the master has conditioned him to what's around the next corner, so there will be no surprises.

The master, while moving the customer to his office, will keep him relaxed with positive thoughts and comments, and above all, won't say any unnecessary things that could upset or confuse the already guarded customer.

When I want my customer to picture owning the product in his mind, all I have to do is look at him and say, "Don't you think about owning this product?" (He will, it works every time.)

—*Michael Schwepp, Wiesbaden, Germany*

Part VII

Act 3:
How Master One Minute
Closers Close the Deal

Customers will motivate themselves if they think
the closer looks up to them.

—Juan Tiamos, Madrid, Spain

In this section of the book, masters tell their one minute closing secrets and share one minute closes that will absolutely generate sales. This is the part of the sales presentation (Act 3) in which the master closer asks his customer to buy or "give the product a try." All through the product presentation, the closer has been aiming toward this one point. It's here that decisions are made, customers get nervous, closers are on edge, sales managers are waiting, and the office atmosphere is thick with anxiety. It doesn't matter how many sales the closer has made, or how good he is, when it comes to this sensitive moment of truth, all involved are alert, poised, and ready to do battle. At this time, the customer should understand the product well enough to make an intelligent buying decision.

Now, keep in mind, reader, the customer might or might not know the price of the product at this point. If the customer knows the price, he's been told by the closer some time during the previous two acts (Act 1 and Act 2) of the presentation. If the customer doesn't know the price of the product as yet, or he doesn't know the financial arrangements available, it's because the master has been deliberately holding that information back until the end of his sales presentation (Act 3) to use as a closing tool. Remember, both of these situations (knowing the price early on in the presentation and not knowing the price until Act 3) can be handled by the closer in about the same manner. What's important is that the closer ask for the order at some point and receive some kind of response. If the customer says, "No, I'm not going to buy," then the closer must keep selling until he feels he has another opening, where he can again ask his customer to purchase.

You either live your dreams, or someone else's.

—*Sharon Bell, Chicago, Illinois*

Note: It is important here to revisit the definition of closing. Closing is a design, tactic, plan, technique, or maneuver with which the master one minute closer puts his customer into a psychological position in which the customer must make a buying decision.

FACT 1. Emotion plus timing equals the right opportunity to ask the customer to purchase

The basic formula for asking the customer to buy is so simple many salespeople overlook it, or make it more difficult than it really is.

Remember, the customer's emotions are everything. When the customer is silently thinking about the product, how it can benefit his family, or how he will look and feel owning the product, he is in the perfect mood to be asked to purchase. To time your approach just right, watch his facial expressions very carefully for any unintentional expressions of comfort, understanding, or satisfaction. When you see these signs, you know that the customer is ready to be asked to buy.

Now, before you actually ask his customer to "give it a try," you must mentally go over a last-second checklist to make sure you haven't forgotten anything. If you silently review this list, you are far more likely to receive a positive response than a negative one.

When you ask the customer to buy, don't hesitate and don't blink.

—*Donti Jakon, Milan, Italy*

FACT 2. The master one minute closer's mental checklist

Mental check A: When the master closer asks his customer to purchase he must make the question soft and sincere, and it must sound "business as usual."

Mental check B: No matter how many objections the customer gives, when the master overcomes them, he must immediately turn right around and ask for the order one more time.

Mental check C: If the master thinks his customer could truly benefit by owning his product, he must decide to stay with the customer until he "closes" him, and that means as long as it takes.

Mental check D: When the master sees the opportunity to close, he should drop everything and ask for the order.

Mental check E: The one minute closer is always calm and in control, never overreacting to anything the customer says or does in response to his questions.

Note: When the master is closing, he must be sure and steady. If his customer witnesses a mood change, senses self-doubt, or notices any silly antics, there will be no sale.

Mental check F: The master must make it easy and comfortable for his customer to buy.

Important note: If a master closer uses any kind of electronic device in front of his customer to calculate finances concerning the product, he must verbally explain to his customer the process in detail each step of the way. This will help the customer understand exactly what the master is doing and will give him some peace of mind. On the other hand, if the closer just punches in some numbers without telling the customer what he is doing or why, chances are the customer will become suspicious, silently questioning how the closer came up with the figures, and will be less receptive to making any kind of buying decision.

If a salesperson is slow-paced in speech and actions, then the customer will mimic that slowness and usually have to think about everything.

—*Reed Spicer, Salt Lake City, Utah*

FACT 3. The master one minute closer asks for the order

When the master closer asks the customer to buy, most customers have three main levels of interest. At the first level, the customer is ready to be asked to buy the product. At the second level, the customer knows all about the product but still needs some last-minute product information. At the third level, the customer understands the product and acknowledges its benefits but still needs time to think things over.

When the one minute closer asks his customer to "give the product a try," to buy the product, the atmosphere has to be "business" sophisticated. The closer can't make any surprising moves, sounds, or shift shocks. He shouldn't do anything until the customer says something first. The master must have complete control at this very delicate moment. Nothing should break the concentration and intensity between the closer and his customer. Once the closer hears his customer's response to "give it a try," he should acknowledge it, conquer it, and close without any shyness or nervousness.

Customers will always pay attention to something that personally benefits them.

—*Aldofo Sanchez, Acapulco, Mexico*

FACT 4. How the master one minute closer conquers customer objections

When it comes to closing the sale, a great many customers will try to outwit the closer's attempt, but it's always the master closer's responsibility to close and win. To do so, he uses the five essential closing truths. These truths will show exactly how the master deals with customer debate.

Closing truth 1

Sometimes the master one minute closer has to trap his customer with his own words, meaning any personal information the customer has revealed about himself during the sales presentation. When the time to close arrives, the closer could and should, if necessary, bring up an earlier-mentioned piece of personal customer information and use that material to his advantage.

Closing truth 2

When the master's customer says "no" to a buying question, it only means he's not quite sold yet on the product. He still has questions. The master will never take the first "no" as the final answer, unless he is convinced his customer can't, in any way, afford the product.

Closing truth 3

When the customer asks a question, the master one minute closer could, if so moved, ask the customer how he himself would answer that question. Remember, the master has to keep control. By letting the customer answer his own question, the master has an opportunity to flatter him by saying, "Mr. Customer, that is what we are going to do," or, "Mr. Customer, my company feels the very same way."

Closing truth 4

There will be times when the master one minute closer must literally make the buying decision for his customer. He has to take his pen, proceed with the paperwork, and start writing up the contract. If the customer doesn't stop the closer, the closer has a deal. All he has to ask for is the customer's signature.

Closing truth 5

When the customer initially says, "I don't believe," or, "I have to think about it," he's simply not sold on the product. These two objections are usually elementary "knee-jerk" reactions and don't mean anything in particular. The closer must ask questions to identify the specific objections the customer has, so that he can address them head-on and eliminate any lingering doubts.

To believe and understand another, one has to share many of the same emotions.

—*Ellen Putman, Los Angeles, California*

FACT 5. Tips for success in Act 3

A. The one minute closer will pay very close attention to how the customer answers him and how he acts. If the master doesn't analyze the customer's answers or actions correctly, he could easily misjudge the situation and design his closing plan incorrectly.

B. The one minute closer will never beg his customer for a sale. The value of one's product and one's self-respect should never be compromised.

C. The one minute closer will never during his sales presentation consider the possibility that he has lost the sale, because his customer can and will detect such self-doubt.

D. If the one minute closer doesn't trial-close throughout his sales presentation (Acts 1, 2, and 3) he risks losing valuable opportunities to close the deal, plus he could lose the customer's attention. The one minute closer will always be sincerely sensitive to his customer's problems and viewpoint.

E. The one minute closer knows he has to be a master senior diplomat and showman, if he ever expects to sell.

F. The one minute closer will listen seriously to everything the customer says, because sooner or later, the customer will tell where he's vulnerable.

G. The one minute closer's sales performance and presentation mean nothing until he gets the customer's signature on a contract.

All one minute closers realize self-confidence births self-discipline, a vital factor when closing.

—*Tomas O'Malley, Dublin, Ireland*

Now, we'll look at some special, tried and true one minute closing tricks and techniques master closers use when they ask their customer to buy the product.

If you truly know your opponent, you know your road to victory.

—*Andrew Chow, Hong Kong, China*

FACT 6. The master closer's eye level

When the master one minute closer asks his customer to purchase, he will intentionally lower his head slightly and get a few degrees below the eye level of his customer. Then, as the customer considers his response, the closer will slowly bring his head up, almost unnoticeably, so his eyes are on the same level as the customer's. Then, right at the exact second when the customer starts to make a sound, the closer will move his eye level up a few degrees above the customer's eye level. At that point, he will keep his head and eyes steady. This very slight head and eye movement is magic. What it does to the customer is surprising. The customer, completely unaware of what the closer is doing, will automatically raise his head and eyes to meet the closer's. This upward physical movement actually encourages the customer to give a positive response. This secret closing technique works, but the master closer has to be very subtle and deliberate in his movement. There can't be any sudden movement that might alert the customer. Remember, many times the body language can actually direct the mind, so use this to your advantage.

The easiest and most satisfying thing a customer can do is talk about himself and his exploits.

—Dan Timerdale, Toronto, Canada

FACT 7. Wearing glasses

If a master closer wears prescription glasses, he will purposely use them to emphasize a point when he feels the time is right. For instance, when the master asks his customer to buy his product, he will slowly take off his glasses and look the customer directly in the right eye. This eye-to-eye contact puts extra pressure on the customer, compelling him to give an answer at that very moment, rather than hem and haw over his decision.

Master closers are professional actors, and when they want to look serious, happy, moody, somber, or overwhelmed, they can do it, and make anyone watching believe.

Customers will always fight harder and debate longer for their own interest.

—*Nick Appadouplis, Athens, Greece*

FACT 8. The hypothetical close

This is a great one minute closer's "debate" technique. If the master senses potential for a heated debate with his customer over some point concerning the product, he will sit back, take a deep breath, and explain his point of view to the customer in a way that keeps the conversation from becoming personal, which might otherwise collapse the deal. For example, the master closer will say, "Mr. Customer, let's say Mr. A was trying to sell some product to Mr. B, but Mr. B wanted to talk to Mr. C, who was his friend, but Mr. C didn't know anything about the product being sold. So, Mr. A told Mr. B that Mr. C would not have that much to contribute to the decision-making process, except to tell Mr. B to be careful. Now, since Mr. B saw the product, can afford the product, and likes the product, shouldn't Mr. B listen to his own reasoning, rather than Mr. C's, since Mr. B will be the person who owns and enjoys the product, not Mr. C?" This simple example might sound silly, but you, the reader, get the point. Whenever there is an opportunity to frame things in hypothetical terms in a closing conversation—a conversation that, if kept personal, might turn ugly—the master closer will do just that. This sales technique saves a lot of wear and tear on emotions and feelings, and it helps bring the customer around to a point of view that he might not previously have been open to.

The master closer will, if need be, use "soft" words to explain and defend "hard" arguments.

—*Brenda Daily, Sydney, Australia*

FACT 9. Stand up to your customer

Reader, this tip can't be stated loudly enough. Customers will not buy from salespeople they don't respect. Don't ever forget, customers will not accept salespeople who are not experts on their products or who show little backbone. Customers are perceptive, and they know that if a salesperson won't stick up for himself, his product, or his company, he sure won't stand by the promises he's made to them. Customers want to purchase from someone who is as good as the product being sold, and if they see a hint of weakness in the character of the salesperson who's trying to close them, they'll lose interest and emotional momentum.

One minute closers are not afraid of their customers. They have to exhibit leadership to direct and keep control. If the customer believes he can walk all over the salesperson or mislead him, it can be guaranteed there will be no sale. If a customer is rude or exhibits hostility toward the closer, the closer can and should cut the sales presentation short. There is no reason for a closer to take any kind of abuse from a rude customer or to waste time attempting to reform him.

Master closers who stand up to their customers will always sell more than salespeople who become docile and let their customers call the shots.

Remember, closers have not sold or converted a customer simply because they have made him silent.

—*Fred Milner, Brisbane, Australia*

FACT 10. Powerful and deadly one minute, one-liner closing statements

The following one minute one-liners are used by master closers for the purpose of getting their customers thinking and excited about the product, or to force a buying decision. These one-liners can be used as one minute mini "closes" or emotion and idea "shakers." (It depends solely on the circumstances.) Such powerful statements and questions have to be delivered with strength, diplomacy, humility, and sometimes a little humor. Unleash one-liners directly and with intent to the customer face to face.

Note: One needn't deliver these one-liners word for word. Rather, one should rework them so they sound natural and applicable to one's product.

For a master closer, simplicity is the trademark of genius.

—*Rubin Hamelpatz, Baden, Austria*

1. "Mr. Customer, did you know that a man's ability to make a decision is based solely on his past accomplishments?"

2. "Mr. Customer, what could I do to help you buy?" The customer says, "Nothing." The master says, "Why?" The customer answers, then the master overcomes the objection and "closes."

3. "Mr. Customer, did you know that all great deeds and advances are achieved by ordinary people who take risks?"

4. "Mr. Customer, tell me something, if you don't have money today because you didn't have money yesterday, then what kind of a track record is that for you to have money tomorrow?"

5. "You know, Mr. Customer, right now you might think you're on a 'path to nowhere,' but with my product you can start being on a path to everywhere, so why don't you give it a try?"

6. "Mr. Customer, let's leave each other better than we found each other; why don't you give my product a try?"

7. "Mr. Customer, if you choose not to decide, you still have made a decision, haven't you?"

8. "Remember, Mr. Customer, if there was no pressure then there would be no diamonds."

9. "Mr. Customer, let's be honest, sometimes you have to buy with your heart and not your head."

10. If a customer says he can't make a decision, the master will either suddenly toss him his pen to catch without warning, or ask him if he wants more coffee. When the customer catches the pen, or says yes or no to the coffee, the master will say, "Don't tell me you can't make a decision; you just did."

11. "Mr. Customer, if my product worked *exactly* as I've told you, would you give it a try?"

12. "Mr. Customer, my grandfather always said that in this world, you have to be your own man. If you just follow in someone else's footsteps, you won't leave any trace to anyone that you've even been around."

13. "Mr. Customer, tell me the truth. If you didn't have to make a decision today, would you buy my product?"

14. "All I am doing, Mr. Customer, is telling you the truth before it happens."

15. "Mr. Customer, I want you to believe in yourself as much as your family and I believe in you."

16. "Mr. Customer, when you buy, I make a commission, which means I get one check. But if I take good care

of you, you'll send your friends to me. And when they buy, I'll make two or three more commissions. So, you see, it behooves me to do my very best for you. That's why I'm offering you the best deal possible."

17. "Do you know what today is, Mr. Customer? Today is tomorrow early."

18. "Mr. Customer, let me tell you something I've learned. When you don't know which road to take in life, any road that looks good to you will do."

19. "Mr. Customer, did you know, if you want to solve any of your problems today, you have to focus on and plan for tomorrow."

20. "Mr. Customer, you're not betting on my company. In all honesty, what you're doing is you're really betting on yourself."

21. "Mr. Customer, I'll tell you what, you want a guarantee? I'll guarantee our product for the next one hundred years if you guarantee me you'll use it for the next one hundred years. Now, let's not be silly, what we're really talking about here is money, isn't it?"

22. "Mr. Customer, if I gave you my product free of charge, would you take it? So, we're only talking about money, aren't we?"

23. "Would you, Mr. Customer, sell me this product?"

24. "You know, Mr. Customer, Abraham Lincoln said, 'Good things do come to folks who wait, but only the things left over from the folks who didn't.'"

25. "Mr. Customer, you say you can't afford it. But I would respond that you can't afford not to have it."
26. "Mr. Customer, if you want the product, we'll find a way that's comfortable for you to own it. All you have to do is say, 'I'll try.'"

Note: If a master closer has a customer who says he can afford the product, and thinks the product is probably a good deal, but won't commit to making any kind of decision under any circumstances, the master can, to see if the customer is only blowing smoke, say to the customer, putting the customer on the spot, "Mr. Customer, I'll tell you what I'm going to do. I know you like my product because you keep telling me so, so I'll make it easy. I'll personally make the down payment for you, and all you have to do is make the monthly payments. Do we have a deal?" Reader, in most cases, the customer will turn red in the face, decline the offer, and start searching for a new excuse not to buy. This is when the closer says, "Mr. Customer, we're talking about money, aren't we?" The chances are good the customer will say, "Yes." Then the master can take it from there and start closing from a different angle. On the off-chance the customer does accept that proposition, the closer must honor his offer and make the down payment, as this technique works only if the closer is willing to put his money where his mouth is.

27. "Mr. Customer, what's the biggest doubt you have about this product?"
28. "Mr. Customer, I know you're a buyer and decision-maker because you have a car, and you have clothes on."
29. "Mr. Customer, tell me, are you hesitant to buy the product or hesitant to own the product?"

30. "Mr. Customer, it's not the measure of money you have, it's the measure of faith you have."

31. "Mr. Customer, you can think about it for a long time, or you can enjoy the product for a long time. It's up to you."

32. "Mr. Customer, you're not buying this product alone. My company is with you. It's a fifty-fifty deal. We'll do our half if you do your half, and that way we both win."

33. "Mr. Customer, when you dream about things you've always wanted but never had, then to obtain them you must do things that you've never done."

34. "Mr. Customer, if you're expecting a miracle, then you had better plan to participate."

35. "Mr. Customer, anyone can say no, because that's easy. From what I know about you, that's just not your style."

36. "Mr. Customer, why didn't you tell me it was the money earlier? You're just like me. You're in the same boat I was in when I bought the product. Let me tell you how I got involved and bought."

37. "Mr. Customer, if you think this product costs too much, tell me, what price would you put on it?"

Note: If the customer gives a price, the closer should say he'll check with his manager, then return to the customer and say, "Okay, you got a deal." In most cases, the customer will make up another excuse. If the customer agrees to the deal, the closer can say, "No, Mr. Customer, I can't do that. My product's worth more than that, but let's keep talking," and then try to close again.

38. "Mr. Customer, you can't make a touchdown sitting on the bench."

39. "Mr. Customer, did you know the only real difference between a rich man and a poor man is the weight of his responsibility? So, Mr. Customer, give my product a try."

40. "Mr. Customer, the product is timeless, but the opportunity to own it is not."

41. "Mr. Customer, life hides its gifts and surprises from those who are afraid to take risks, and my product is not a risk, so you can really have your cake and eat it, too. Why don't you give it a try?"

42. "Mr. Customer, I'm not supposed to do this, but you take the contract home, look it over, and I'll be by tomorrow and pick it up, then we can talk more."

Note: Watch the customer try to get out of this situation. All the master has to do is say "It's the money, isn't it?" and then close.

43. "Mr. Customer, why do you think so many customers before you have purchased?"

44. "Mr. Customer, I meet folks like you every once in a while. You're broke today, and tomorrow you'll be a millionaire. Let my product help you with tomorrow."

45. "Is it possible, Mr. Customer, that you've fought, worked, and struggled through life so long that you don't know how to do anything else? Let my product help make a difference in your life."

46. "Mr. Customer, my product tells the world who you are, without your having to say a word."
47. "Mr. Customer, don't you feel that you've earned the right to own this [my] product?"

Behind every word spoken live seven thoughts.

—*Berret Campbell, Dublin, Ireland*

FACT 11. The master closer's fourteen most powerful one minute closes

Presented here, for the first time in print, are the fourteen best one minute closes used by master closers from around the world. Bear in mind, these closes are not for beginners. These techniques are for the best by the best, and they work under any sales condition.

Note: Reader, every single close described in the following pages can be delivered in one minute or less. The main thing the closer must remember is to always ask for the order after each close, saying, "Mr. Customer, why don't you give my product a try?" The closer should never stop asking the customer for the order. In all honesty, it will always, with very few exceptions, come down to a money problem. If the closer can just work out the finances, he or she will get a sale.

A salesman takes his time to calculate, plan, and prepare to close, a master closer just "closes."

—*Jan Multon, Vancouver, Canada*

1. The "you can afford it" close

This close is the simplest, most understandable and powerful close there is for its particular purpose. If used under the right circumstances, this close will get a sale or get a reaction from the customer every time. Designed to work on a customer who wants the product but keeps telling the master closer he can't afford it at this time, this close is so basic and to the point that many closers forget to use it.

How to use the "you can afford it" close

When a customer says to the master closer that he likes the product, but can't afford it at this particular time, the master should quickly reply, "Mr. Customer, I know you like the product, and I know you'd like to own it. Let's just see if you really can afford it."

Note: The master closer had better be bonded close enough to the customer to freely discuss his personal finances. If this relationship of trust doesn't exist, this close probably won't work.

At this time the master closer should get a blank sheet of paper—the back of a contract, order sheet, or worksheet would work—and say to the customer, "All right, Mr. Customer, let's put down in black and white your monthly expenses. Let's see if you really can't afford the product."

Note: At this moment, before the master closer starts to record the customer's monthly expenses, the master must secretly jot down his product's monthly cost at the top of the sheet. If, for example, the product's monthly payment is three hundred dollars, that is the amount the master would write down. After writing down the three-hundred-dollar monthly payment, unbeknownst to the customer, the master starts itemizing, with the customer's help, of course, and in a soft voice (so it's only between closer and customer), the customer's monthly expenses, right below the three hundred dollars.

For example, the closer would list house payments, car payments, insurance, medical, and food and utilities bills. When the total monthly expenses are lined up and added with the secret three hundred dollars included, again without the customer's knowledge, the master closer should say, "Mr. Customer, in total, your monthly costs are around three thousand dollars. Is that pretty close?" Remember, reader, the master wants the customer to think and see for himself that the three thousand figure is accurate. So the customer is in effect acknowledging that he cannot afford the product. After the customer agrees the dollar figure that the closer has come up with is pretty close to his monthly obligations, the master closer will say, "Mr. Customer, do you think we could add another three-hundred-dollar payment to your monthly outlay?" At this point, the customer will think he's off the hook and say with conviction, "No way! I told you I can't afford the product. I'm pretty well strapped right now, as you can see." This is when the master closer pulls the plug. He says to the customer, "Well, Mr. Customer, congratulations, you *can* afford this product, because I've already included the three-hundred-dollar payment in your three-thousand-dollar-a-month budget, so welcome to the club." The master closer should immediately turn the piece of paper around so the customer can see the expense list for himself. At the same time, the master should stick out his hand for a handshake agreement. Most likely, the customer will be shocked, because he knows his ploy has been exposed. There is nowhere for him to go except to sign to the contract or start scrambling for another excuse not to buy. This close will catch the customer completely off guard. But, instead of a triumphant "I told you so," the master closer should calmly start writing up the purchase agreement, acting as though this kind of financial problem is solved every day and as if it's a done deal. This close will work every time, if the situation is right. It will take a little practice on the closer's part to get this close down smoothly, but once it's mastered, sales will go up overnight.

In sales, if you're afraid to be wrong, then you'll never be right.

—N. Ming Lu, Hong Kong, China

2. The "B.A.D." close

This close is designed to make one very important point, and that is to show the customer he should spend his hard-earned money on his family and other worthwhile investments instead of on excessive insurance policies that eat up money unnecessarily. This exercise requires a little simple drawing, which always helps capture the customer's attention and gets him accustomed to seeing the closer's pen. This close might seem too animated for some, but it's clean, makes sense, and gets sales.

Special note: This close uses insurance as the bad guy, but this close can be redesigned for other products.

How to use the "B.A.D." close

When the master closer has a customer who likes the product, can afford it, but won't make a buying decision, he can turn to this close not only to illustrate a point, but also to get the customer thinking in a different direction and from a different point of view. This in turn only makes the customer more receptive to purchasing the closer's product. Here's how it works: Right after the customer tells the master closer he's not going to make a buying decision, the master closer will take out a blank sheet of paper and politely ask the customer to watch and listen to what he has to say. Then, the master will first, on the left side of the blank paper, draw a little "stick" house. The house will only be one story, meaning two walls and a pitched roof. After the master has drawn the house, right underneath it he will draw a little car—a small box with two circles. Third, the master closer will draw, right below the car, a little stick figure. So, if someone is looking at the paper the master has been drawing on, he or she will see on the lefthand side first a house, beneath it a car, and below the car, a person, all vertical and in a neat row. After the master has silently drawn these three symbols in front of his customer, he will look up from the paper and into the customer's right eye and say, "Mr. Customer, let me ask you a question. Do you have insurance on your home?" The customer will answer "yes." Then the master says, "Well, for you to collect any insurance money on your home, your home has to what?" The customer will say, "Burn."

Note: If the customer doesn't answer, the closer will answer for him and say, "Burn." Now, when the customer says, "Burn," the master closer will print the word "burn" next to the stick house on the right.

Then the master closer will ask his customer a second question as he moves his pen down the paper an inch or two. This time, pointing to the little stick car, he asks, "Mr. Customer, for you to collect insurance on your car, you must have a what?" The customer will say, "Accident."

Note: Again, if the customer doesn't answer, the closer will have to answer for him and say, "Accident." Then the master closer will print the word "accident" next to and to the right of the little car. Remember, reader, the word "accident" is printed directly below the word "burn."

Now, right after this question about the car is answered, the master poses the final question to his customer.

He will say, as he once more moves his pen down one or two inches to the stick figure. "Okay, Mr. Customer, for you to collect insurance money on a person, then that person has to do what?" The customer will answer, "Die." Then again, the master closer will print the word "die" or "death" next to and to the right of the little stick man. The word "die" is printed directly below the word "accident," which is printed below the word "burn." Once this is done, he will look up at his customer and say—as he circles the first letters (B.A.D.) of the three words—"Mr. Customer, you have been spending a lot of your money for protection against B.A.D. things that might happen. Why don't you reward yourself and your family and start spending some of your money on good and fun things—things you and your family can enjoy? My product is just that sort of thing. This product is something positive for you and for your family's future. All I need is for you to give it a try. I need your name right here next to mine." Reader, the customer will sign the contract. This close is an easy way to make and illustrate a very important "good" statement.

If a salesperson only knows two or three closes, he or she knows nothing.

—*Sarah Bohn, Cape Town, South Africa*

3. The "did the salesperson lie?" close

This close has to be rehearsed between the master closer and his sales manager or a fellow closer before the master tries it out on a customer. It can be quite effective, but it must be acted out by the master and his partner with complete confidence. If, for one second, the customer thinks this close is a "put-on," the sale will be lost. In this unconventional close, the customer is led to believe that he is not the party under the gun, but instead is only sitting on the sidelines, in the role of a witness. In this unique but deadly close, the customer doesn't find himself in the middle of the close until it is too late.

How to use the "did the salesperson lie?" close

When the customer refuses to close and sign the contract, the master closer should excuse himself from the closing table to go get his sales manager or associate closer for this prearranged closing exercise. When the master returns to the closing table with his colleague, and all the introductions have been made, the colleague will turn directly to the master closer, ignoring the customer, and ask him the following questions, in a tone so pointed the customer feels as if nobody remembers he's there. "Mr. Master Closer, did you tell Mr. Customer about the special options on our product?" The master answers obediently, "Yes, sir, I did." Then the manager or fellow closer asks, "Did you explain to Mr. Customer everything about our special warranty?" "Yes, sir, I did," responds the master closer, as he looks to the customer for confirmation and support. The manager or fellow closer again asks, "Did you take the time to show him all the advantages of owning our product?" The master closer answers, "Why yes, sir, I certainly did." At this point, the customer may start nodding in the affirmative, trying to support the beleaguered master closer, who is now getting an embarrassing lecture. Then again, the manager or associate closer will ask, "Did you tell Mr. Customer about our financial setup and contract arrangements?" The master closer again answers, "Yes, sir, I covered all of that information." Now, at this point, the customer should be ready to defend the poor, kind master closer, because he is beginning to feel guilty that his new friend is getting in trouble for not closing the deal. Once more, the manager or fellow closer asks, "Did you also discuss with Mr. Customer our company's reputation and its performance history?" "Yes, sir, I honestly did. You would have been proud of me if you were here listening," answers the master closer. Then, out of nowhere, the manager or associate closer says sternly to the master closer, "Speaking of honesty, Mr. Master Closer, did you lie to Mr. Customer about anything?" The master closer answers, "No, sir, I assure you that I didn't." Then the manager or fellow closer, acting satisfied with master closer's answers, should wait a dramatic few seconds, then turn straight to the customer and ask in a puzzled but firm voice, "Well then, Mr. Customer, why didn't you buy?"

Boom!!! A direct hit! The customer who was thinking he was out of the picture and has been sitting there feeling empathy for the humbled master closer is now directly in the spotlight. He now has his mouth half open in surprise, not knowing quite how to respond.

Off balance and off guard as he is, the customer will most likely stammer and blurt out some spontaneous truth, that in turn is his real excuse for not buying. Once the master closer hears the real objection, he can go ahead, overcome it, and close the deal.

Note: This kind of double-team close is very effective. The customer has been set up and forced, by a surprise attack, to admit either that he truly can't afford the product or that there is not really any good reason why he doesn't go ahead with the purchase.

Show me a master closer who keeps failing and I'll show you a master closer who has just given up.

—*Evola Lenvamekk, St. Petersburg, Russia*

4. The "one dollar versus one-hundred-dollar" close

This close is used when the customer tells the master closer he can't make a decision. This close will immediately show the customer that he can make an on-the-spot decision. It is designed to make a high-impact impression on the customer, and it does just that. Reader, this is a very simple, fast close, so don't try to make it complicated.

How to use the "one-dollar versus one-hundred-dollar" close

When the master closer has a customer who says he just can't make a decision, that it's not in his character to jump at anything, or that he always takes his time, this is the close to use. When the customer says, "I can't make a decision today," the master closer should pull out of his pocket a one-hundred-dollar bill and a one-dollar bill, then hold them both up, one in each hand, in front of the customer and say, "Mr. Customer, would you trade me one dollar for a hundred dollars if there were no strings attached, no gimmicks?" Now, if the customer says nothing, the master will answer for him and say, "One dollar for a hundred dollars, no strings? Well, of course you would do that." The customer will agree verbally or nod in agreement. This is when the master says, in a don't-play-games-with-me voice, "Mr. Customer, don't ever tell me again you can't make a decision, because you just did. You know what you just told me? You told me two things. First, you told me you can make an on-the-spot decision, and second, the reason you made that decision is that you know the value of one dollar and the value of a hundred dollars. You understand and believe their value because you positively have that information in your head. So, now I know you can make a decision if you have enough information. Now, let me explain more about my product so you can make a positive buying decision." At this point, the customer will say something, and what he most likely will say is the true reason he's reluctant to purchase. Reader, never forget, in most every case, with a few exceptions, it will be the money. This close will make the customer smile and come clean, or it will mildly upset him, which only means the master is getting closer to the true reason the customer won't buy.

Never get into an argument with a customer who has nothing to lose.

—*Masi Alomon, Tangier, Morocco*

5. The "you're not approved" close

This close is specifically designed to put a particularly difficult customer on the defensive by using the basic science of reverse psychology to play on the customer's ego. If applied correctly, this technique will make the customer feel uncomfortable and feel that he is not qualified to own the product and therefore feel an urgency to own it. The master closer who uses this close had better be a good actor and had better be prepared for an argument. Remember, reader, even though this is a hard close, it will get sales.

Note: This is another close that involves the master and a fellow closer to implement. In other words, it's a double-teamer.

How to use the "you're not approved" close

When a master closer is getting nowhere with an apathetic, rude, or arrogant customer, it is a good time for the master to call in his sales manager or fellow master closer to execute this high-impact close. Now, this is how this close works. The manager or fellow closer will meet briefly at the closing table with both the master and the customer. Then he, the fellow closer or manager, will excuse himself from the group and disappear into his office or out of sight. Two to four minutes later, the manager or fellow closer will reappear with a serious and downcast air about him. Solemnly, the manager or fellow closer takes his place at the closing table and declares, "Mr. Customer [use first name, if possible], I've got some disappointing news for you. Please forgive me and the company for wasting your time here today. Just now, when I went back to my office, I checked out your credit rating, and your current financial condition isn't quite strong enough for you to purchase our product under our present purchase and ownership plan. I apologize we didn't catch this earlier. I really hope you can forgive us for wasting your time."

Immediately after this blow to the customer's pride is delivered, the manager or fellow closer should casually turn to the master closer, who is sitting next to the customer, sigh, and say, "Sorry, Mr. Master Closer. I know you wanted this sale, too." Now, the stunned and insulted customer is likely to attack the bad credit remark and challenge the master closer, manager, or fellow closer on his subtle condescension. The manager or fellow closer should act as if he is on the side of the customer and say he will be glad to recheck the source of his information to confirm it is indeed correct or incorrect. At this point, the angry customer will be upset about this disclosure of his confidential credit rating, so he'll start talking, and the more the customer talks and acts, the more information and ammunition he is spouting to the master closer, valuable information the master can use to discover and break down the customer's deep and true purchasing objections. Then, when the honest objections surface, and they will, the master should explain how they can be overcome and add how much he appreciates the customer, no matter what some silly credit report states. Now, at this exact moment, the manager or fellow closer, who has been sitting at the closing table, listening to the master overcome the customer's true objections, should gracefully, at the perfect time, stand up and declare that he will personally see to it that finances and ratings won't stand in the way of the customer's owning the product. He, the manager or fellow closer, should immediately stick out his hand for the customer to shake, acknowledging the sale has been made. This close gets sales, but it had better be acted out professionally, or things could get rough.

Note: If necessary, the master could also add, "Mr. Customer, we have our own financing, and believe me, our company hasn't gotten so big and successful by saying 'no' to people."

6. The "board of nails" close

This close will work wonders if the story below is told in a soft and sincere tone by the master closer, and of course, properly adjusted to the particular product being sold.

How to use the "board of nails" close

When the master closer has a reluctant customer, one who won't budge and shows no sign of moving toward a sale, this is a perfect opportunity for the master closer to use this emotional and logical story close.

With the customer and master sitting at the closing table, all attention is trained toward the master closer when he says the following:

"Mr. Customer, let me tell you a story. There was a man having coffee one morning in his kitchen, just minding his own business, when his wife walked in and suddenly, out of nowhere, said to him, 'You know, you're mean to me. You treat me badly and say hurtful things to me.' The husband looked up from the breakfast table and said, 'What? What do you mean?' the wife responded, 'You have been mean to me all this past year. I was up late last night thinking about it and I'll prove it. I'm going to put a big plywood board on our kitchen wall, and every time you're mean to me this coming year, I'm going to hammer a nail into the board and I'll show you just how hateful you are.' In no time a year had passed, and one morning the husband entered the kitchen and found his wife standing there pointing to the board on the wall, saying, 'Look at that board. I told you that you were mean to me!' The husband looked and studied the board for a few minutes and saw nothing but solid nails. Even on the edges of the board, there were nails. In fact, the board couldn't hold another nail. The husband suddenly realized his wife was telling the truth about his being so mean, so he said, 'You know, you're right. I have been mean to you this past year. I'll tell you what I'm going to do. This next year, to make it up to you, I'm going to be especially kind and every time I am, I'm going to take one of those nails out.' The wife agreed, and the subject was dropped. One year later, the husband was sitting at the breakfast table, proud as punch, waiting for his wife to enter. She came in for her coffee, and he said triumphantly, 'Look at that board now. There is not a single nail in it. See, I told you this past year I was going to change.' The wife looked at the board, and sure enough, all the nails were gone. But then she pointed to the board and said, 'Yes, that's true, all of the nails are gone, but just look at the board.' As he looked, he saw a board full of old nail holes and claw hammer marks where he had pulled the nails out. There were warped areas and splinters everywhere. The board was nothing but an ugly and mangled piece of wood. The wife said, 'True, the nails are gone, but the scars and destruction marks are still there.' Well, Mr. Customer, I'm telling you that you don't have to live like that. You and your family, like everyone, have a dream board, but something keeps coming up in your life, and every time it does, you take a nail out of that dream board. Then one day you look and you see nothing but scars, splinters, and lost dreams. Mr. Customer, with my product, you can have some of those dreams back. You can have what you've always wanted instead of a dream board full of empty holes. That, Mr. Customer, is what my product can do for you and your family." After the master closer tells this story, he should give the customer a minute to let it sink in, then he should say, "Mr. Customer, I need your name right here" (on the contract). The master closer should immediately stick out his hand for the customer to shake in agreement. This storytelling close will work miracles, but it must be told with sincerity and emotion. The customer has to feel the master closer is on his side, making a genuine illustration for the benefit of his family's personal needs, wishes, and wants.

Closers cloaked in reason survive, while closers cloaked in passion live.

—*Deck Delane, Liverpool, United Kingdom*

7. The "three reasons" soft close

This closing technique is simple and it gets the customer thinking positively. It also prompts the customer to get involved with the product.

How to use the "three reasons" soft close

When the master closer has done just about all he can to persuade his customer to buy, and the qualified customer still won't budge, the master can use this closing method to nudge the customer a lot closer to signing the contract. After the master has used nearly everything he can without blowing up the deal, he can politely excuse himself from the closing table to "check on some late date inventory" and say to his customer, right before he leaves, "Mr. Customer, I'll be a few minutes, but while I'm gone, why don't you do me a favor and write down three reasons you would buy my product." The customer, in most cases, will do as suggested. When the master returns, he can go over the three reasons, build positively on each one, re-emphasize important points the customer left out, and then continue to close, guided by this new information. This simple little closing maneuver will give the master a "road map" leading straight to the customer's heart, and a sale.

If a salesman questions faith and hope, then he had better accept poverty.

—*Stanley M. Cooper, Atlanta, Georgia*

8. The "What would Jesus do?" close

This close is designed to get sales by overcoming nearly any excuse a churchgoing customer might come up with. Reader, this close is not sacrilegious or disrespectful to heaven in any way whatsoever. It is a one minute close that will make a very strong and lasting impression on the Bible-toting customer who keeps thinking up reasons not to buy, while letting pride get in the way of telling the master closer the true reason, which, of course, is most likely money. This close has to be delivered tactfully and with self-confidence and strength. It should never be used by a new or timid salesperson, or the consequences could be severe. The customer could get so upset that a fight might ensue. This close works, but the master closer had better respect the customer and the customer has to have respect for the master, so he'll listen and understand that this close is being used in a friendly manner, but with a business meaning.

How to use the "What would Jesus do?" close

When the master closer has a "Sunday go to meeting" customer who likes the product but keeps coming up with one excuse after another not to buy, the master could use this close. When doing so, the master closer must be telling the absolute truth about everything concerning the product, and the master must totally believe in the product he's selling. This technique will not work if there is any doubt whatsoever in the master closer's mind about the product's worth or value.

After the master closer has heard a number of excuses for not buying from this type of customer—for example "I have to think about it," "I have to check with my friends or lawyer," or "I'll talk to my accountant first"—he, the master closer, will say this to the customer: "Mr. Customer, I know you're a good person, you go to church and take good care of your family. I know you like my product, but let me ask you this. You keep telling me you have to check with your lawyer or accountant before buying, and I appreciate that, but you are a Christian, and Christians try to act like Jesus, don't they? Isn't that the whole meaning of Christianity? To be kind to everyone, giving, loving, and acting like Jesus? Well, Mr. Customer, I've read the New Testament, too, and let me tell you this. I'll give you this product free of charge. It won't cost you a thing, and we'll remain friends, if you can tell me anywhere in the New Testament where Jesus said, 'First, let me talk to my lawyer,' 'Let me see what my friends think,' 'Let me check with my accountant,' or, 'I have to think about it.' Mr. Customer, show me one place in the Bible where Jesus couldn't make a decision on his own, and I'll give you my product absolutely free."

BOOM!!! The customer is stunned. The master closer has made such a strong and truthful point, the customer doesn't know what to say. So, immediately after this statement is made, the master closer should, with the greatest look of sincerity he can muster, say to the customer, "Mr. Customer, we want you to be an owner. You're the kind of person who makes our product great. It's important for us to have wonderful owners like you. So, do like I did, give our product a try, and I promise you, you won't be disappointed." Reader, in nine out of ten cases, the customer will start to relax, enjoy the master closer's sincerity, and sign the contract. Remember, if the product isn't on the up and up, and it's not a good deal for the customer, heaven help the poor salesperson who tries to use this close.

No salesperson ever became a master closer by chance.

—*Santiago Lamous, São Paulo, Brazil*

9. The "you believed" close

This close will make the customer reflect that maybe he is being silly by waiting to buy the product at a later date. The master closer must convince the customer there is no benefit in waiting, and any delay is merely due to his nervousness about having to make a buying decision "today." This close will work, but the master must deliver this close with sincerity and calm so the customer gets the point the first time around. The master closer has to convince the customer that erring on the side of caution is still erring, in this particular case.

How to use the "you believed" close

Note: Remember, reader, any close presented here can be redesigned for any particular product or sales situation, and if the basics stay the same, they will produce sales.

First, we must set the stage for this excellent close. In this illustration, we'll use a customer who is expected to make a buying decision at a real estate development. The customer has been invited to a resort for some gift, but in accepting the gift, he is obligated to tour the property with a real estate closer. This "you believed" close is a great close to get the customer who is somewhat interested, but scared of making a decision to buy. The master closer, after all else has failed, should say the following: "Mr. Customer, let me ask you something. When you received my company's invitation to visit our resort, you believed we would honor that invitation, didn't you? Sure you did, because you're here, aren't you?"

Note: Always give the customer a second or two to agree, then move on.

"After you drove your family here to visit us, you believed that you would receive a gift, correct? And you did get the gift as promised, didn't you? Mr. Customer, you were aware you would have to take a tour of our property and you did, didn't you? In other words, Mr. Customer, you believed everything we told you and never doubted us, because you're actually here, true? Well then, Mr. Customer, let me ask you this. If you believed everything we've promised so far, and everything we've said has been true, then why don't you trust us and believe us the rest of the way? This reminds me of the champion swimmer who swims halfway across a lake and then says to himself, 'I can't make it,' so he turns around and swims all the way back to the shore where he started from. Now, Mr. Customer, does that make any sense to you? Of course it doesn't. All I'm asking you to do, Mr. Customer, is believe us the rest of the way. You've believed us so far, so don't doubt yourself, and don't doubt us. Mr. Customer, I need your name right here on the contract." At this time, the master closer should either stick out his hand for an agreement or go ahead and sign the contract himself, then hand the pen to the customer to sign. This close is powerful if delivered in a caring, understanding, and confident tone.

The master closer knows that one's appearance and attitude can overwhelm facts.

—*Kevin Vocevic, Prague, Czech Republic*

10. The "seven directors" soft close

This is another of those closing techniques that will lead the master closer straight to a close. This exercise is simple, understandable, and painless. This closing method is designed to help the master diagnose his customer's weak and strong points better. It gives the master closer great personal information about the customer so, in turn, he can adjust his closing battle plan to get a sale. There is not a customer alive who, when asked in a kind and sincere manner, would not acquiesce to this easy request.

How to use the "seven directors" soft close

When the master closer and customer are sitting at the closing table and the master feels the time and situation is right, he'll think of some excuse to leave the table for a few minutes, but before he goes, he will say, "Mr. Customer, we've been together now for more than an hour, and I've found you to be a unique and strong individual. I want you to do a favor for me while I'm away from the table. Just for my own curiosity, here's a piece of paper and a pen. Would you write down seven people in the history of the world who you would have on your board of directors to run and manage your personal life?" In most cases, the customer will happily consent. When the master closer returns to the closing table, he can examine the seven individuals and get a very good "inside" look at the character and mental makeup of the customer. The master can go over the list with the customer, endorsing and congratulating until the closer sees the customer's true personality emerging. He then uses the insights he's discovered to his advantage and continues to close in a fashion that complements the customer's nature. Reader, this little exercise might sound very elementary, but it works. This closing technique guides the master straight to the emotional target and bull's-eye of the customer's hot buttons.

When I know I'm positively correct in doing something, there are not risks.

—Maria de Allano, Naples, Italy

11. The "I'll be back" close

This is a special, simple close that works. It will make any customer who says, "I'll be back," look and sound foolish. Any master closer who uses this close can, after it has been presented to the customer, go ahead and write up the deal. Most customers who hear this close will break down and tell the master closer the true reason he doesn't want to buy "today." Then, of course, the master can take that "real reason," overcome it, and get a sale. Reader, this one minute close is a plain-Jane, uncomplicated one, but the results are amazing. The closer just has to say it in a lighthearted and "surely you jest, Mr. Customer" manner.

How to use the "I'll be back" close

To use this close, the master closer has to have built up a good relationship with his customer. Now, this close could be used on any "be back" customer, but it works a lot better with a customer who likes the closer, and respects him. When the master closer has a customer who "kind of likes the product" or "likes the product," or one who seems to have nothing to say except, "I'll be back," the master will use this one minute close. This is how it works. If the master closer says to his customer, "Give my product a try," and the customer just smiles and says, "I'll be back," the master closer says, "I'll be back? Do you, Mr. Customer, really know what that means? It's like saying and seeing thing backward, like back to work, back problems, back pay, back bills, back of the class, backwater, back row, back wall, back stairs, backache, backbreaking, backside, back up, back down, back then, back when, back there, back page, back lot, back track. Mr. Customer, you've got your thinking all wrong. Everything with 'back' is negative. You need to change your attitude so you'll be thinking positive. So, come on, start thinking forward instead of thinking backward. You know you want this product, so what we're really talking about is money, isn't it?" The customer, in most cases, will say, "Yes." Then the master closer can go in and work out the deal. There is one more thing the closer could say after he swamps the customer with "backs." He could say, "Mr. Customer, I don't want you to think like that: Go forward, back is the past; change your direction in life and go toward something that will help you become successful." This is a fun close, but it is also very effective and does make an impression on the customer, and that impression won't go away easily. Reader, believe it or not, this close will get sales.

Success in sales depends heavily on a trained and disciplined mind.

—*William Hewett, London, United Kingdom*

12. The "three stolen things" close

This is another close the master closer uses when he has a Bible-toting, churchgoing customer. This customer is a good person who just won't make a buying decision. This type of customer is a little nervous, and can't, for the life of him, get motivated. The master closer must use this close with sincerity and kindness, showing he understands the customer's position, but would gently like to make a very important point, one the customer will take to heart and remember.

How to use the "three stolen things" close

If the customer is a conservative, religious person who likes the product, but doesn't want to make a decision about buying today, the master closer can use this "story close" to help push the customer to do something besides just sit there and say, "Not today." After the customer says he can't make a decision, the master closer should say, "Mr. Customer, let me tell you a story.

Remember, in the Old Testament, when Lucifer was cast out of heaven with his legions of fallen angels? Well, one day, down in Hades, Lucifer was walking around this big dark chamber when he was approached by five of his lieutenant angels. They gathered around Lucifer and asked this question. 'Lucifer, besides us, what else did you steal from heaven that would help us imprison the world and capture mankind?' Lucifer just smiled and said, 'Oh, I only stole three things, I didn't need anything else. Besides, I've got you and the other fallen angels. So, I think, with you and the three things I pilfered, we can own and control the whole world in no time.' Puzzled, the lieutenant angels looked at each other in wonder; then one of them said, 'All right, we give up, Lucifer, what three things did you steal from heaven that will make our job so easy?' Lucifer said, 'Well, if you really want to know, I stole one thought, one emotion, and one word.' The lieutenants again looked at each other, and one said, 'Okay, you win. What's the one thought you stole?' Lucifer said, 'I stole the thought "impossible."' Then another angel lieutenant said, 'All right, what was the one emotion you stole?' Lucifer turned to him and said, 'I stole the emotion "fear."' Then, after several quiet minutes, another fallen angel said, 'Lucifer, we'll never guess what the third thing was. You said it was one word. Well, tell us what that one word is.' Lucifer smiled, looked directly at the fallen angel who had asked the question, and answered, 'tomorrow.'" Immediately after the master closer tells this story, he should look directly at the customer, wait one minute or less, then say, "Mr. Customer, I need your name right here, next to mine." The master closer immediately hands the pen to the customer to sign the purchase order. At this point, the master should act as if this is a done deal and just assume the customer will sign. In reality, the customer will ask a few more questions, then, when satisfied, he'll sign the order, or the customer will give a nervous laugh and try to think of another excuse not to buy. If the customer comes up with another reason for not purchasing, the master closer will overcome that objection and ask for the order one more time. Now, this back-and-forth contest could go on and on, until the customer finally wears out and tells the master the true reason he won't make a decision. When that happens, the master closer can readjust his closing plan, if necessary, do his magic, and get the deal. Remember, no customer can outwit or outsmart a true master closer.

The closer who even thinks about retiring, begins to die.

—*Hanns Burgen, Stockholm, Sweden*

13. The "pressure, resale" close

This is a great one minute close to use on any customer who thinks the master closer is using too much sales pressure. This close is designed to turn a customer who is getting upset into a cooperative customer the minute the master closer explains his high-pressure techniques. This close, like all the closes described in this book, has to be delivered by strong and intelligent people. There is no room for mistakes or salespeople who don't have the will and character to get their point across in a controlled and confident fashion. Customers need to have a director (master closer) who knows how to orchestrate a presentation on time, in time, and with a balance of tone and facial expression that all who observe will appreciate, respect, and understand.

How to use the "pressure, resale" close

There are many times when the master closer finds himself "grinding" on a customer who has the wherewithal to purchase, but just can't or won't make a buying decision. This kind of customer likes the product, but won't be pushed, pressured, intimidated, or embarrassed into buying. This customer, in truth, is one tough character. He's smart, has money, and won't be cornered by some slick salesperson. When the master closer finds himself with such a customer, and in a situation in which the customer says, "I'm through, you're using too much pressure on me, and I'm not going to buy," the master closer has a great card up his sleeve. The master can use this closing card at any time he feels the conditions are right, and believe it or not, reader, get a sale. This is how it works. When the customer says, "Stop, I've had enough, too much pressure," the master closer will say, "Wait just a minute, Mr. Customer. Let's say you bought my product, and over the next two years we shared phone calls, Christmas cards, and visits. We became good friends. Then, one day, you call and ask me to sell your product, the one you originally bought from me. Of course, being friends, I agree. Then, sometime down the road, I have a customer sitting in front of me and I'm trying to resell your product and this customer keeps saying, 'I've had enough, I'm not buying,' or, 'I'll be back.' Then you tell me one thing, Mr. Customer, exactly how much pressure do you want me to use to resell your product? Do you want me to sell your product for you, or just let every customer I talk to walk out of the sales office and hope that maybe someday, some customer I let go will return and buy? You tell me, Mr. Customer, how much pressure should I use to sell your product so you and I can make some money? You know, Mr. Customer, what you're really seeing here is a demonstration of how hard I'll work for you in the future. So, let's be realistic. You like my product, you can afford my product, so all I need is your name, right here next to mine. Mr. Customer, just give it a try." Reader, in most cases the customer will do an about-face and sign the contract. To use this close successfully, the master closer has to be firm, businesslike, and totally devoted to his product and the good it will do for his customer. This is a "big dog" close that only works when delivered by a truthful, charismatic, and powerful master closer. This close will make a master closer a lot of sales, deals that other salespeople would have missed.

The more I learn about sales, the more I want to learn, and maybe someday, I'll obtain wisdom.

—*Otto Leipkken, Berlin, Germany*

14. The "thought" close

Reader, every master closer in the world wants to discover the one magic close that will get sales every time it is used. In reality, all customers are different, and so are all sales situations, and to find such a close would be almost impossible. But this one minute close is an exception. The "thought close" is about as close to that magical close as one can get. This is one of the most powerful closes on earth. In fact, it might possibly be the greatest. The author has heard closes from around the world, and this close, the "thought close," has no equal. This close, when mastered and tweaked for a particular product, is positively deadly. No customer can fend off its message or influence. Any closer who uses it had better be telling the truth about his product and had better be dedicated to his product. This close is too good to be used in any sales situation that is not honorable. To explain and demonstrate this close, we are going to use an automobile as our product example, but this close can be used for real estate, insurance, stocks, bonds, home improvements, or any product. All the master closer has to do is rework it for his industry and adjust it to his personality.

Note: Before now, only five master closers in the world knew about this close. Once they started using it, their sales went up 50

*percent. This close can be used on any customer, no matter what
the excuse is for not buying. This close should never be tried or
used by rookie salespeople.*

How to use the "thought" close

This is how it works. This one-minute close is strictly
a "talking close." Now, when all seems lost, the master closer says, "Mr. Customer, let me ask you a question. Are you going to be a medical doctor tomorrow
night? The customer will say, "No." If he doesn't answer,
the master will answer for him and say, "No." Then the
master will ask the customer a second question: "Are
you going to be an international professor of law tomorrow?" Again, the customer will say, "No." Then the
master will ask his third and final question: "Are you,
Mr. Customer, going to get up in the morning and be
an astronaut?" Again, the customer says, "No." Then the
master says, "Mr. Customer, do you know why you're
not going to be any of these three professionals? Well,
it's because you weren't supposed to be. The thought
of being a doctor, professor, or astronaut wasn't in your
head. You, Mr. Customer, do believe in a greater power,
a supreme being, if you will, don't you?" Most customers
will answer, "Yes." Then the master closer says, "Now,
that supreme being will test you and put you through
tough times to make you stronger. But, Mr. Customer,
your maker wouldn't put a thought in your head saying
you're going to be a great lawyer someday so that believing that thought, you go to law school and as soon

as you get your law degree, you hear all of the voices of heaven laughing and saying it was all a joke. Your maker wouldn't intentionally tease you like that, would he?" The customer answers, "No." The master closer continues, "Mr. Customer, you're an expert mechanic because maybe your father was, or you knew from an early age you were good with your hands. So, today, you're a professional mechanic because you had that thought in your mind. You knew you would be good in that profession because you thought it, true?" The customer will likely answer, "Yes." The closer continues, "Remember, Mr. Customer, all of those little sayings like, 'If you think you can you can?' Well, they're right."

Then he says, "Mr. Customer, let me ask you one simple question. How many times have you thought about driving up to your home in a brand new automobile? How many times have you thought about going on a trip or riding around town with your family in a new automobile? You know, Mr. Customer, that thought has been in your mind because it's supposed to be there. It was put there for a reason. I didn't put it there. Remember, where there's a will, there's a way, and that's why you, Mr. Customer, are here in my office right now, because you are supposed to be." Then the master shuts up. Now, reader, the look on the customer's face is unbelievable. He has a blank look, but you can hear his mind working at a thousand miles per hour. Suddenly, all of the dots are connecting. A light bulb just went on. The customer will have this funny and puzzled look for about five to seven seconds. That's when the master closer sticks out his hand for an agreement to purchase, and the customer will, on impulse, shake it. The deal is done. All that has to be taken care of now are some details and paperwork. The customer has purchased the new automobile.

Reader, this "talking close" is a surefire strategy. The reason this close is so powerful is that the customer *has* been thinking to himself about a new automobile, and he now understands that he's been thinking of it for a reason. All of a sudden, everything makes sense to him. He actually sold himself by believing in his own dreams, and all the master did was pave the way so he, the customer, could look at the product being sold from a different and very personal angle. This phenomenal close, when used in the right situation by a master closer, with strength and conviction, disregarding any money problems, will make any customer who hears it buy. This close works because the customer hears the truth, knows it for the truth, and realizes in his own heart that everything the master closer said is the truth.

If you, Mr. Customer, want to stop making financial mistakes, then you need to stop trying to succeed.

—*David Olsan, New York, New York*

This concludes our look at certain closes and mini-closing statements. The closing exercises and techniques detailed here work. They will get sales. All the closer has to do is get comfortable with them, use them in harmony with his or her personality, and enjoy the success. If these one minute closes and one-liners are delivered with conviction, there is no limit to a closer's earning potential.

Part VIII
How Master One Minute Closers Think and Act After the Sale

The master closer will always give a humble
customer the recognition he deserves, the
recognition others have deprived him of.

—*Winston O'Donalley, County Cork, Ireland*

After the master one minute closer either closes the deal or misses and says good-bye to his customer, his emotions will be running extremely high. Before he meets his next customer, he will go somewhere alone and try to walk off his energy to some degree. If he sold the customer he was last with, he will use that positive momentum to meet, and most likely sell, his next customer. If, on the other hand, he missed his last customer, he must "shake it off" and get mentally prepared for his new customer. Under no circumstances can he meet and greet his next customer with a look of defeat on his face. Remember, customers are very attuned to any negative emotions the closer might exhibit. Reader, the master closer is a professional performer, and his strength lies in his ability to regroup and rebound. The next customer needs a closer who is running on one hundred percent positive energy, and the master is one of the few people on earth who can and will deliver.

Master closers start at the top, then work their way up.

—*Betti Tonialla, Rome, Italy*

FACT 1. Thank the customer

This is plain old common sense. After the customer agrees to purchase, the master closer will thank the customer for his business and tell the customer he appreciates his trust. This "thank you" has to sound and feel like a normal, everyday event. The customer must not get the idea this is the first sale the closer has ever made. That will only unnerve the customer, who is already sitting on pins and needles. The master will be appreciative, but not abundantly overjoyed or ecstatic. Control is the key. Remember, business as usual should be reflected in the closer's eyes and actions.

Note: Reader, after the deal is made, the master closer will "shut up," and he won't say another word about the product. If he volunteers extra information, there is a chance he'll say something the customer doesn't like or understand and the whole deal could go down the tubes. Now, if the customer still has some questions after the contract is signed, the closer will hear the customer out fully, and then say, "Mr. Customer, why do you ask?" Remember, let the customer explain his question in total so the closer will know exactly how to answer without going into a lot of detail, which could also kill the sale. The closer will be precise, concise, and straightforward in his answer, never giving any room for further speculation or deliberation.

Now, to help illustrate the point about not going too overboard on thanking the customer for his purchase, there is an old Chinese story that should be told.

A long time ago, there was a Buddhist monk traveling home from a small village in China. The monk was days away from reaching his home when he came to a wide, dangerous river. Being alone, he decided the only way to cross the river safely was to build a raft. The monk tied bamboo poles together with vines, selecting the biggest shoots he could find, and after ten long days of laboring, he finally had a raft large enough, one he felt was secure and reliable. Dragging the heavy raft to the edge of the river, he carefully launched it and was very pleased with himself, because it floated, and was well balanced. After a few minutes of admiring his accomplishment, he boarded the raft, shoved off, and three miles down the swiftly running river, after some nerve-racking close calls, was safe and dry on the other side. The monk was so happy and thankful to the raft for working so perfectly, he decided to tie vines around it and take it with him. After dragging, pushing, and pulling the heavy raft down the small trail for about a mile, he stopped, looked at the raft, and thought; "True, this raft saved my life and got me across the river, for which I'm forever thankful, but this thing weighs a lot and pulling it down this path is killing me." So, the monk simply thanked the raft and left it there, traveling the rest of his way home happy and burden-free.

Remember, reader, you can overdo anything and ruin it, so just be polite to your customer, thank him for doing business, and proceed as normal.

If a customer wants the product badly enough, he or his family will find a way to purchase.

—*Frank Rhinehart, Wasserburg, Germany*

FACT 2. The expensive pen

To help ensure and solidify the deal, the master closer will hand his personal pen to the customer to keep immediately after the contract has been signed. The closer's pen has to be of some value, and one the customer would use and be proud of. The pen can't have the company logo or any product information on it. It must look like a pen the customer went out on his own and bought. Now, what this small gift does to the customer is beautiful. The customer will be touched, but will also likely play around with the pen, try it out, inspect it, and admire it. Keep in mind, reader, as the customer is handling the pen, the contract could be drawn up, or if there is a lull in the closer-customer conversation, the pen will take the customer's mind off the "dead time." Plus, it will give the customer something that is tangible, so he won't be just sitting at the closing table, thinking about the money he just spent on the product. The "expensive pen" exercise works wonders on any customer, giving him the feeling this is a special time to remember and appreciate.

Note: If this pen technique didn't work, then the president of the United States wouldn't hand out pens when he signs important documents.

After the sale, you should always give the customer something extra and unexpected.

—*Cid Puckett, Washington, D.C.*

FACT 3. Ask customers why they bought

The master closer will ask his customer, after the contract has been signed, in a friendly and lighthearted way, why he bought the product. The customer will give two or three answers, but will always leave out two or three very important points. This gives the master closer the opportunity to remind the customer of certain benefits the customer might have forgotten, plus it gives the master time to reinforce and support the customer and his buying decision. The master closer knows it's very important to "hold hands," or, in other words, comfort the customer with reassuring dialogue, after the sale.

Reader, nothing will upset a customer more than seeing the closer lose interest in him the second the contract is signed, or watch the closer take congratulations from other salespeople in the sales office, as if the closer hasn't sold in months. Master closers will, if possible, walk the new owner to his car and wave good-bye. They will not just let the customer walk out of the sales office alone. First of all, that's not professional or polite, and second, the new owner could start a conversation with other folks who might not be so satisfied. The master leaves nothing to chance, nor should he.

When I think I don't need advice is usually when I need it.

—Charles Moody, San Francisco, California

FACT 4. Ask for help

The master one minute closer is the person who is at the top of his profession, a true pro who is streetwise and holds a doctorate in human behavior from the world university. Master closers are not stupid, so when they want advice or help from another closer from whom they know they can learn, they will ask. In the sales business, anyone can discover a new sales method, technique, or close from someone else. It makes no difference who teaches or who learns, sales is a sharing of knowledge. Any closer who, because of pride, refuses to ask for help when his numbers are down is playing a fool's game. There is not a master closer alive who would not go out of his way to help and encourage another closer if asked.

This world needs great characters, risk takers, free

thinkers, and daredevils, men and women who don't follow, but lead.

In fact, this world would still be in the Stone Age if it weren't for the courageous souls who had the faith to give all, blindly believing in what they thought was right, and master closers are in every respect that kind of individual. Thank heaven for all those who see further than others, believe more than others, and have the good sense to ask for directions when lost.

Note: There is a very wise saying in the legal profession; "The letter of the law ensures civilization, while the spirit of the law defines civilization."

The same formula holds true in the sales profession: "The letters of closing are ensured by psychological techniques and mechanical steps taken to get a sale, while the spirit of closing is defined by the sincerity, trust, and integrity used throughout the closing process."

Sometimes you have to make yourself humble to make yourself great.

—*Walter Gates, Miami, Florida*

Conclusion

Truth, passion, and faith have never failed me.

—*Beverly Ann Reece, Scottsdale, Arizona*

All master closers around the world know the sales profession is a noble business, and if you're going to be successful in this business, you have to be noble. When studying to be a one minute closer, the most effective and honest training available is to actually get out in the world and close deals. When mistakes are made, one shouldn't worry, because mistakes teach more lessons than success. Remember what was said in the Author's Note: "Learn everything you can, then pass that learning along." Well, that philosophy is the author's true feeling. If one ceases learning, one cannot adequately teach. Heraclitus said, "Nothing endures but change." He was right. The world changes every single day, but the basic wants and needs of people always stay about the same. Master closers learn new things relating to sales all the time, and this, coupled with their ever-present passion, allows them to honorably sell their products to people who have dreams, feelings, every emotion imaginable, and humanistic and culture-blending factors that nothing in this "high-tech" world can compete with. This is the master one minute closer's world, and it is always waiting and depending on his enthusiasm. He never gives in or surrenders to mediocrity. The master closer also knows, deep down in his heart, that God never has created and never will create a life that is destined to fail. The master one minute closer understands, when all else seems to fall apart, he can, in prayer, reach toward a strength that is always there, and never find or receive an answer that is superficial, foolish, or empty. Reader, the world is waiting, expecting, and needing the unique energy all master closers possess. Master one minute closers have that wonderful ability to change people for the better, and every time they do, their actions are never forgotten, actions that silently keep slipping in and out of heaven.

Finally, every master closer alive realizes that if he fails to use his God-given talents for the good of all, or takes his gifts for granted, that saddest of failures, that disregard for such great blessings, will be echoed forever throughout the halls of remembrance.

I made a stand today, and after some time, no one tried to move me.

—*Bill David Benton, New York, New York*

About the Authors

JAMES W. PICKENS is one of the most dynamic and respected sales educators in the world. He and his work have been featured in *Publishers Weekly* and *Success* magazine. Past clients include Disney, IBM, Sheraton, Marriott, Hilton, Westin, Mirage, GM, and Ford. His audio books are in-flight on American Airlines and he has been featured on countless talk shows around the world.

Pickens was born in New Orleans and educated at Rogers High School, Arkansas, the University of Arkansas, and the University of Colorado. After serving in Vietnam, he formed his own business, becoming a multimillionaire by the age of thirty-seven. Pickens is the author of *The Art of Closing a Deal, The Closers, More Art of Closing Any Deal*, and *Cleopatra's Secrets of Negotiation and Persuasion for Women*. Combined these books have sold several million copies worldwide.

Pickens has one daughter and two grandchildren, and he resides in Dallas, Texas, Acapulco, Mexico, and Arizona.

JOSEPH L. MATHENY is a nationally known and respected business media personality who specializes in teaching sales closing methods and techniques to professional sales people. He has personally trained some of the top master closers in the world and his thirty-five-year success record and achievements have been heralded and recorded in countless business publications. Matheny is dedicated to making good closers great master closers.